TERRORISM

A Reference Handbook

TERRORISM

A Reference Handbook

Stephen E. Atkins

CONTEMPORARY WORLD ISSUES

ABC-CLIO

Santa Barbara, California
Denver, Colorado
Oxford, England

Library of Congress Cataloging-in-Publication Data

Atkins, Stephen E.
    Terrorism : a reference manual / by Stephen E. Atkins.
      p. cm.—(Contemporary World Issues)
    Includes bibliographical references and index.
    1. Terrorism—Handbooks, manuals, etc. 2. Terrorism—
Bibliography. 3. Terrorists—Directories.
    I. Title.
    HV6431.A87 1992   909.82—dc20   92-28530

ISBN 0-87436-670-4 (alk. paper)

99 98 97 96 95 94 93 92   10 9 8 7 6 5 4 3 2 1

ABC-CLIO, Inc.
130 Cremona Drive, P.O. Box 1911
Santa Barbara, California 93116-1911

This book is printed on acid-free paper ⊖.
Manufactured in the United States of America.

Contents

Preface

Terrorism, in all of its manifestations, continues to plague contemporary international affairs. Almost weekly a terrorist act takes place somewhere in the world. While no region has proven to be immune, terrorism has become endemic in the Middle East and South America. Since 1945 an estimated near 30,000 terrorist activities, or almost two incidents a day from 1945 to 1992, have been carried out. It is this worldwide use of terrorism by individuals attempting to transform the international order, or to overthrow the state, that makes this subject so important for everyone to understand.

Few citizens of the United States have been directly affected by terrorism, except for the occasional American casualty in an aircraft bombing or the victim of a hostage incident; but Americans are still horrified by the specter of terrorism. Americans tend to identify with victims more than terrorist causes. News reports and special precautions at public buildings and airports are the most overt evidence that terrorism constitutes a continuing domestic threat to Americans. To maintain vigilance against terrorism, the American taxpayer has had to foot the bill for these security precautions. A myriad of antiterrorist legislation has been passed by Congress to protect American against terrorism, but the American public still feels insecure.

Part of this insecurity is that the American public knows so little about terrorism and terrorist organizations. The mass media reports only a fraction of terrorist activity because information is hard to uncover and because the belief is widespread that publicity only encourages terrorism. A few experts provide most of the research on terrorism and their conclusions are scattered among many publications. The U.S. government alternates between passivity and panic over the prospect of domestic terrorism and with a staunch counterterrorism philosophy toward international terrorism. This dearth of information means that teachers, writers, students, the concerned public, and government leaders have been left with only scanty reliable information about terrorism.

This lack of information about terrorism has made it difficult for the concerned citizen to understand the philosophy and nature of the differing brands of terrorism. Though different forms of terrorism often coexist in different regions of the world, terrorism is acknowledged to be a threat to the international order, or to the existence of a state's regime. Adherents of terrorism embrace this threat as a valuable political instrument to initiate widespread political change.

This book fills the information gap about terrorism and is intended for teachers, students, government officials, and the general public. It tries to be objective in an area where objectivity is rare. An introductory essay places terrorism in its political context. Terrorism has gone through several stages and this essay looks at these stages and the tactics used by various terrorist organizations. A chronology follows and is intended to give the reader a sampling of the most significant terrorist incidents in the last hundred years. Special emphasis has been placed on showing the variety of groups resorting to terrorism and their specialties. Biographies of terrorists come next, and this chapter gives an insight into the psychology of the individual terrorist. Good biographical information on terrorists is always difficult to find because they are reluctant to provide accurate information. Terrorist leaders are reluctant to give the authorities or anyone information that might lead to their capture or curtail their operations. The next section contains a lengthy list of terrorist organizations in operation since 1945. This section provides the most accurate and up-to-date data on these ever-changing organizations. Next is a relatively short section on documents dealing with terrorism. Emphasis here is less on government agreements than on demonstrating the terrorist mindset. Finally, a select annotated bibliography, organized by topic, provides the reader with opportunities for further research in the field of terrorism. The index provides help in accessing the large number of titles of organizations and complex names of individuals, as well as access to subtopics of terrorism.

My perspective on terrorism has been formed by my experience as a researcher on international security issues. I was the Arms Control and Disarmament Bibliographer at the University of Illinois at Urbana-Champaign for six years before moving to Texas A & M as the head of collection development at the Evans Library. For the last three years I have been a member of the board of directors of ACCESS: A

Security Information Service, which specializes in providing information on international security issues. My military duty in South Vietnam in 1968 revealed the difficulty of low-intensity warfare—typical of what governments face in dealing with terrorism.

Terrorism is one of the major unresolved issues of the twentieth century. Until other channels of political recourse can be opened up, terrorism will continue to be one of the instruments used by the dispossessed. Use of terrorism by the state to control its population in some respects is even more insidious than international terrorism. International attention has mostly been directed toward countering international terrorism, and attention needs also to be directed toward terrorism by states.

The reader will find that terrorists believe in a cause and will die carrying out their missions, and those opposed to terrorism maintain just as staunchly that no cause justifies terrorism. This book presents the kind of information that may provide the reader with a means to see all sides of the issue.

I want to thank my family—Susan, Stephanie, Jordan—and my friends for their support.

1

Introduction

TERRORISM DATES BACK TO BIBLICAL TIMES and before, but the kinds of terrorism occurring since World War II have attracted a great deal of attention among governments, scholars, and the general public. The postwar struggle for national liberation by ex-colonies and the subsequent military and political weakness of the colonial powers gave impetus to the rise of terrorism. Along with this deterioration, the chaos of the postwar era and the unfulfilled aspirations of countless nationalities provided a ripe environment for discontent. This discontent, the long stalemate among the superpowers, and the international weakness of the new states have made terrorism a weapon favored by the underdog. An additional factor has been the discontent among intellectuals in both the industrialized countries of Western Europe and in the Third World over the slowness of social progress. This discontent, sometimes attributed to a combination of vengeance for perceived social wrongs and despair over the failure of the masses to act in their own best interests, has created a generation of intellectuals and their followers ready to resort to terrorism.[1] These intellectuals consider terrorism to be part of a continuum that runs from conventional war through guerrilla warfare, insurgency, sabotage, and terrorism. Any group with a grievance against the dominant society can find terrorism a way to publicize its existence and advance its cause. Assassinations, bank robberies, bombings, extortion, and kidnappings have all become part of the terrorist arsenal. While the victims may not sympathize, terrorists claim that they are in continuous war against society and the international order and that violence is justified.

This "war" has had many unforeseen results. Terrorists advance a cause, and part of their strategy is to destabilize society enough that the repressive nature of the state will assert itself. These terrorists believe that such repressive policies will provoke enough popular protest so that societal transformation is possible, or that the state will grant independence to its separatist regions. In actuality, except in the isolated cases of Cuba, Israel, and Algeria, terrorist efforts have not yielded the desired result. Instead, repressive regimes in the Third World have crushed revolutionary terrorism by adopting national terrorism. In the more advanced industrialized countries, counterterrorist tactics have been well developed, and the chances that social revolutionaries will attain power or force the creation of separatist states are remote.

Terrorism in the Middle East has always been different because of the support it receives from sympathetic states in the Arab bloc. Arab nationalism and the Palestinian cause have not always proved compatible, however, and Israeli intransigence prevents any progress regardless of the intensity of the terrorist campaign. There is little hope for peace or for a curtailment of terrorism unless a settlement is found that brings the Palestinians into the international order.

Throughout the world, terrorism still remains a threat to the established political order in the 1990s, but it is likely to be less intensive than it was in earlier years. Nevertheless, as long as any group can find reasons to declare war on the international order or an individual state, terrorism will always be an available weapon.

Many of the terrorists and terrorist organizations discussed in this book have long disappeared, but they are included nonetheless because terrorism has developed an elaborate mythology. Terrorists adopt a mind-set that requires both a history and a pantheon of martyrs. Virtually every new terrorist movement identifies itself with a previous incident, individual, or group. Some terrorist organizations have borrowed their names, organizational structures, or leadership styles from previous groups. Reference to a former terrorist organization gives a solid clue to the orientation of a new group of terrorists. It is for these reasons that terrorism must be studied in its historical context.

Philosophy and Theory of Terrorism

Definitions of terrorism are both difficult and notoriously inaccurate. Every effort fails because terrorism means different things to different people. A double standard of terrorism exists because, as one scholar in the field notes, "Some forms of political violence are described as terrorist, while others that bring greater human loss do not invite that label."[2] A sampling of some of the more popular definitions of terrorism indicates the difficulty of exact definition:

> An organized pattern of violent behavior designed to influence policy or intimidate the population for the purpose of influencing government policy.[3]

> Symbolic action designed to influence political behavior by extranormal means, entailing the use or threat of violence.[4]

> The use of force, violence, or threats thereof to attain political goals through fear, intimidation, or coercion.[5]

> Almost all illegal acts of violence committed for political purposes by clandestine groups.[6]

> The premeditated, deliberate, systematic murder, mayhem, and threatening of the innocent to create fear and intimidation in order to gain a political or tactical advantage, usually to influence an audience.[7]

> Any violent act against innocent people intended to force a state, or any other international subject, to pursue a line of conduct it would not do otherwise.[8]

> Politically motivated violence engaged in by small groups claiming to represent the masses.[9]

> The resort to violence for political ends by nongovernmental actors in breach of accepted codes of behavior regarding the expression of dissatisfaction with, dissent from, or opposition to political goals endorsed by the legitimate government authorities of the state.[10]

Despite the differences in language and sometimes prejudicial choice of terms, each of these definitions is oriented around two concepts: the use of violence and a political aim behind the terrorist act. The political use of violence to provoke fear is a tactic that has been used by left-wing and right-wing terrorists as well as authoritarian and totalitarian governments. Another aspect to the understanding of terrorism is the importance of the terrorist's use of surprise.[11] Surprise gives the terrorist the advantage of picking the time and place to strike. Fear and surprise are both key tactical concepts used by terrorists. Finally, terrorism is an inexpensive way for terrorists to initiate war against society. The similarity between war and terrorism has caused at least one expert to classify terrorism as a form of warfare.[12] It costs the authorities much more to combat terrorism than it does the terrorists to conduct a terrorist campaign.[13]

So much attention has been given to studying the characteristics of terrorism that it can now be better understood. One such study lists seven specific characteristics of the political use of terror:

1. The systematic use of murder, injury, or threats to realize a political objective such as revolution or repression.[14]
2. An atmosphere of fear, coercion, and intimidation.[15]
3. The inherent indiscriminateness: indiscriminate attacks are made on noncombatants (soft targets)—no one in particular is the target; no one is safe.[16]
4. Its unpredictability: the individual is unable to avoid injury or death.[17]
5. Its denial of all rules or conventions of war.[18]
6. The savage methods of destruction used, such as car bombs, mail bombs, double bombs, and mass murder.[19]
7. The moral justification for acts of terrorism, found in the group's political philosophy.[20]

While the characteristics stated above are universal among all terrorist organizations, the goals of left-wing terrorism differ markedly, because the terrorists intend to bring about a social revolution by overthrowing an existing regime. Consequently, most left-wing terrorists subscribe to the following goals:[21]

1. To provoke government overreaction, especially indiscriminate reaction.
2. To overthrow oppressive regimes.
3. To cause isolation and demoralization of individuals, creating an atmosphere of anxiety and insecurity.
4. To release prisoners and publish manifestos.
5. To immobilize security forces.
6. To obtain financial resources in order to purchase weapons and explosives.

These goals are intended to destabilize a regime so that a popular movement can obtain power in the state. The most famous examples of the types of organizations that employ these tactics are the Red Brigade in Italy, the Red Army Faction in Germany, and the Action Directe in France.

Right-wing terrorist groups have a different orientation from the left-wing groups. They are also unhappy with the direction that society is taking, but they tend to want to return to an earlier and happier time. Sometimes members of military and police feel so threatened by left-wing terrorism that they form or join these right-wing terrorist organizations. This has been the case in several terrorist groups in France, Italy, and Spain. An estimate has been made that right-wing terrorists in Italy carried out more terrorist acts and killed more people between 1969 and 1975 than their left-wing counterparts.[22] These individuals conduct terrorist campaigns to destroy what they consider the enemy within. Often right-wing terrorists isolate Jewish and/or immigrant populations for their attacks. Racism and fear of communism seems to be common characteristics of these groups. These right-wing groups, however, are not above training alongside left-wing terrorists, and sometimes they also adopt the same targets.[23] However, they belong mostly to small groups and their activities have not posed serious threats against democratic government.

Many repressive regimes, especially in the Third World, have a right-wing philosophy, and these regimes use right-wing terrorist groups to suppress social reformers and intellectual dissidents and to retain power. In Latin America and Central America, civil war sometimes breaks out between the left- and right-wing terrorist groups. Often these right-wing groups attack prominent intellectuals and members of labor unions and peasant cooperatives. These terrorists are frequently protected by the state's internal security forces, because they are carrying out state policy.[24]

Some of the American racist right have adopted terrorism for the same reasons as their compatriots in Europe and Latin America. These individuals feel that they have to cleanse the country of "undesirables," such as Catholics, Jews, Blacks, and Hispanics. They are heavily armed and most of their followers live in the western United States. Several of these groups have paramilitary organizations ready to defend themselves. The only group to engage in widespread terrorism, however, has been Robert Jay Mathews' group, the Silent Brotherhood. This group of fewer than 15 activists has lost its influence since the death of Mathews and the long prison terms of his followers. Other groups make an appearance, but none of them has resorted to terrorist activities on a broad enough scale to be worth mentioning.

Despite provoking attention and causing enormous loss of life and property, terrorism has had limited success in achieving its objectives. Of the more than 200 terrorist groups documented between 1945 and 1991, and terrorist acts numbering nearly 100,000, only three states have been created or fundamentally changed by successful terrorist action: Algeria, Cuba, and Israel. These cases developed in very different historical contexts. Two of them—Algeria and Israel—gained freedom from colonial powers. The Cuban case was closer to a social revolution than the others, and it has also been classified as a guerrilla war more than a terrorist campaign. Many of the same arguments that attribute success more to low-insurgency warfare than to terrorism also apply to Algeria. These arguments do not apply to Israel, but terrorism alone did not win independence for the Israelis. Most scholars of terrorism agree with Walter Laqueur's statement that "not a single government has been overthrown as a result of terrorist action."[25]

Richard Rubenstein has postulated four conditions necessary for the success of terrorism:[26]

1. The society is already disrupted by economic crisis or war.
2. The activists are supported by fellow members of some ethnic, religious, or national group.
3. The activists' aims are limited to destabilization of the regime in power or opposition organizations.
4. Their opponents lack the finances, the will, or the political strength to conduct an extended counterterrorist campaign.

These restrictions make terrorism a risky and futile tactic in any usual scenario to overthrow a regime or state, because the probability of all these conditions being in place is remote.

State-Sponsored Terrorism

Some states have become infamous as sponsors of terrorism. These sponsor states have made it difficult for international counterterrorism policies to work, because the terrorists are always able to find a safe haven. The U.S. Department of State has classified Cuba, Iran, Iraq, Libya, North Korea, South Yemen, and until recently the Soviet Union and some Eastern Europe countries as the leading exporters of terrorism.[27] Syria was dropped from this list as part of the diplomatic effort to free Western hostages in Lebanon.[28]

Various degrees of state sponsorship of terrorism can exist:[29]

1. A state uses terrorists to commit acts as the representative of legal or de facto state agencies.
2. A state employee's use of unofficial agents that are "organized, equipped, commanded, and controlled by the state."
3. A state gives financial aid or weapons to the terrorists.
4. A state provides logistical support (training of terrorists).
5. A state consents to terrorists finding sanctuary before and after performing acts of terrorism.

Two types of states sponsor terrorism: those states with an ideological commitment to the cause advanced by the terrorists, and those states with an interest in destabilizing the international order. Sometimes a state will share both characteristics. These maverick states will sooner or later run into conflict with the great powers or suffer an embarrassing rebuff from the international community. This fear of a rebuff has been the reason that some Middle Eastern states have become more reluctant to accept landings of hijacked airliners since the 1970s.

Most of the Middle East states fall into the ideological supporters camp. These states have supported the Palestinian cause because of a common political heritage, geographical proximity, a shared religion, and desire for political survival. Consequently, these states have continued to provide Palestinian terrorists with financial support, facilities for the terrorists to train and launch terrorist operations, and, finally, safe havens for terrorists at the end of their missions. Any group that advances the Palestinian or Arab cause can claim such support from these states. Several states, such as Algeria, Libya, and Syria, have taken the lead in sponsoring terrorism against supporters of Israel. Other states, such as Egypt, Kuwait, and Saudi Arabia, have been more circumspect, but they too have long supported Palestinian terrorism. Lebanon is a special case because the lack of a viable government has made it a staging ground for all types of terrorism.

Libya, Syria, and Iraq have created separate terrorist organizations to advance their own foreign policy objectives.

Besides political support, several Middle East states have been active in funding terrorist organizations. Even conservative states, such as Kuwait and Saudi Arabia, provided the Palestine Liberation Organization (PLO) with operational funds for several decades, but the recent Persian Gulf War lessened some of these nations' enthusiasm for this support. Other backers, such as Libya's Muammar Qaddafi, have released funds inconsistently or to specific groups and persons who might carry out their policies. In the PLO there has been frustration with Qaddafi's level of support.[30] Information has surfaced over the last decade that the PLO has become a wealthy organization that is no longer dependent on subsidies from Arab states. It has been pointed out that as the PLO's wealth has grown, its dependence on terrorism and military force has declined—its leadership unwilling to jeopardize the new-found wealth.[31]

The former Soviet Union and, before unification, East Germany, were the most active practitioners of terrorism as a destabilizing element to gain foreign policy advantages. Many of the early Palestinian terrorist groups sent their followers to the Soviet Union for training in political awareness and irregular warfare. Patrice Lumumba University in Moscow was a popular place for Third World countries to educate future leaders, and these students provided a source of possible recruits for further training by the KGB. Some of the Palestinian graduates of Lumumba University assumed leadership roles in terrorist groups during the 1960s and 1970s (a boom era for such groups). Several of the terrorist groups eventually established their own training facilities. Soon organizations as diverse as the Irish Republican Army (IRA), Basque Nation and Freedom (Euskadi Ta Askatasuna [ETA]), and the Red Army Faction had members training in these camps. Soviet sponsorship of early terrorist activity was designed to advance its interests in the Middle East and prevent the United States from gaining a political foothold with the Arab states. This activity seemed to decrease in the 1980s as the Soviet leadership became more uncomfortable with its sponsorship of terrorism. The collapse of the Soviet economy in the early 1990s ended even the pretense of Soviet aid for terrorism. With significant internal problems facing them, it is unlikely that Boris Yeltsin or other leaders of the newly formed republics will support terrorism in the near future.

East Germany followed the lead of the Soviet Union, except that it had more contacts with European terrorist groups. Many left-wing terrorists used East Germany as a haven between terrorist campaigns. The reunification of Germany ended this cozy relationship, however, and European terrorists have had to find other sanctuary. Finding these terrorists has been difficult because the East German secret police protected them. The opening of police files in 1991 has produced more information about East German involvement in terrorism.

Some critics of the theory of state-sponsored terrorism charge that emphasis on state support for terrorism distorts the debate on ways to control international terrorism. They argue that terrorism has a broader appeal than solely as an instrument of sponsoring states' international policy. In contrast, adherents of the theory of state-sponsored terrorism hold that terrorism can be managed by muzzling the sponsoring states, because it fits "into a familiar spectrum of international conflict and national security threats."[32] Recent U.S. administrations have strongly supported this view.

State-sponsored terrorism can have hidden dangers, as when the following situations occur:[33]

1. Terrorism escalates into a war between two or more small countries in which major powers feel obligated to intervene.
2. A major power takes unilateral military action in response to what its leaders consider provocation or to what they feel affects their vital interest, and this action destabilizes the international order
3. A state overreacts to terrorism, thereby undermining democratic institutions and causing foreign policies to be either overturned or transformed.

In all these cases, the responses may make the cure worse than the disease. State-sponsored terrorism is still present in the 1990s, but its sponsors are more circumspect than in the past. The former open tolerance of Arab states to Palestinian terrorism, for example, has become more selective. This selectivity has grown partly because of the political environment spawned by the 1991 Persian Gulf War.

Terrorist Organizations

Any study of terrorism is complicated by the seemingly endless proliferation of terrorist organizations. Many of these organizations have strict discipline among the rank-and-file members, but internal dissension among the leaders over strategy, tactics, targets, and/or personalities has caused most of them to split into competing factions. Sometimes these factions have broken away to form separate terrorist organizations. Organizational literature defines the behavior as *exit* or *voice*.[34] Voice is the articulation of complaints to redirect the group toward an alternate course of action. Exit is the act of leaving the organization to join a rival group, or splitting off to create a new group. Despite efforts to control dissidents, no organization can avoid either voice or exit.[35] Terrorist organizations have been notorious for both voice and exit. Leaders in terrorist groups are usually designated because they helped found the group or because their authority is generally recognized.[36] Neither of these reasons prevents a challenge to the leader over strategy, tactics, or even personality. Disagreements have resulted in behavior ranging from verbal attacks to open warfare between former allies. It is not unheard of to have death sentences pronounced and executions carried out between the competing groups. The most extreme case remains the Japanese Red Army, whose leadership ordered 14 members executed over ideological issues. Another current example is the open warfare of the Abu Nidal Group against the PLO leadership.

Terrorist organizations are built around a common cause, but these causes differ significantly among groups. The record of terrorist activity since 1945 indicates that four types of terrorist organizations exist: separatists, national revolutionaries, international revolutionaries, and right-wing vigilantes. Each type of organization attracts a different kind of terrorist.

Separatists form terrorist organizations to break away from an existing state, either to form a new, independent state or to unite with another established state. These separatists are usually an ethnic group, united by a common language, with a historical claim on a specific geographical region. They sometimes evolve from a political party that has been unable to reach the goal of making an independent homeland. These groups organize in order to attract attention to their cause and gain converts, as they are unable to operate without some popular support. Some of the terrorist organizations that advance a separatist agenda are the IRA, IRA-Provisional Wing (Provos), ETA, Popular Front for the Liberation of Palestine (PFLP), and PLO. These are some of the most violent terrorist groups, employing assassination, bombing, hostage-taking, kidnapping, letter bombing, skyjacking, and any available means to advance their separatist cause.

National revolutionaries are driven by the desire to bring about a social revolution in a single state. They attack the institutions of the state, especially the police and the judiciary, in an effort to discredit the institutions and to provoke a hostile response. Part of this philosophy is the belief that the more savage the response, the greater the possibility of gaining adherents to the revolution. Many of these terrorists have Marxist-Leninist leanings, and they often employ the examples of the Cuban and Russian revolutions. At the same time the terrorists work to destabilize the regime, they act to build popular support. One of the tactics of this type of terrorist is to project a "Robin Hood" image by seizing goods from the rich and distributing them to the poor.[37] A similar tactic is to kidnap a foreign businessman and use the ransom to stop layoffs or plant closings. Both the Tupamaros of Uruguay and the Argentine People's Revolutionary Army (ERP) practiced this method on occasion.

Though social revolutionaries may work to destabilize specific regimes in a particular countries, they also cross international lines in an effort to reshape the international social order. These revolutionaries may use terrorism to advance the cause of world revolution. Sometimes these terrorists are content to operate in a single country, but the social revolution in the host country is often regarded as merely a first step toward the international social revolution. These revolutionaries rationalize their violence in these terms:[38]

1. Society is sick and cannot be cured by half measures of reform.
2. The state is itself violent and can be countered and overcome only by violence.
3. The truth of the terrorist cause justifies any action that supports it. While some terrorists recognize no moral law, others have their own "higher"morality.

The European Red Brigade, Red Army Faction, and Action Directe are all examples of social revolutionary terrorist organizations.

On the opposite end of the political spectrum, vigilante terrorism attracts conservative and right-wing groups that use terrorism to destroy the threat to the established order. Most of these terrorists are disturbed by the current social unrest and want a return to a safer, simpler world. They adopt the strategy and tactics of the enemy by using assassination and bombing as a weapon, believing that the government has failed to control terrorism through legal means. These movements draw many adherents from the police and the military. Brazil's Death Squad and Argentina's Triple A are examples of vigilante terrorism. French and Spanish police have been active in right-wing organizations formed to fight against left-wing terrorism and against others that the police consider undesirables. Other right-wing groups are attracted to a cause, such as anti-Semitism, and their terrorism is directed toward Jewish or Israeli targets. Many of these groups retain links to movements of the past (e.g., Nazism and Fascism), but others have a more anti-communist and anti-modernism orientation and avoid reference to right-wing organizations of the past.

Terrorist Incidents

The most tangible notice of the existence of a terrorist movement is the terrorist incident. A secret organization may exist but until it commits a terrorist act, it is often little more than a political debating society. The desire by inexperienced terrorists to gain publicity quickly for their cause is the reason why the first acts of terrorism by a group are usually botched. Only after the terrorists gain expertise and establish their priorities do they become a significant threat to anyone but innocent bystanders.

Terrorist incidents follow certain patterns. Experience with terrorism over the last half-century has allowed such incidents to be classified into 11 types:[39]

> 1. Kidnapping—A prominent government official or
> businessman is seized and held until a set of demands is
> fulfilled. Kidnapping has long been one of the more
> popular techniques used by terrorists. Several terrorist
> groups have specialized in this type of action, including
> the Tupamaros of Uruguay and the People's
> Revolutionary Army (Ejercito Revolucionario des Pueblo
> [ERP]) of Argentina. Kidnappings reached an all-time
> high in 1975, but since then kidnappings have lost some
> of their appeal to terrorists.[40] Part of the reason has been
> the increase in protection afforded potential targets. The
> lack of political success by the various Iranian-backed
> Shi'ite terrorist groups in their kidnapping of Westerners

in Lebanon in the late 1980s and early 1990s has also made this tactic less popular.

2. Barricade and Hostage—Hostages are secured, but the terrorists stay at the scene of the incident to negotiate terms. High casualties and a lack of success have made this method less attractive to terrorists since the 1970s. Only terrorist groups with a secure political base, such as the Palestinian terrorist organizations, can use this technique successfully. The most notorious use of this type of operation was by Black September at the 1972 Munich Olympics.

3. Skyjacking—An aircraft filled with passengers is seized and the passengers serve as hostages until demands are met. In the period between 1968 and 1979, 102 major aerial hijackings took place. Some Palestinian terrorist groups, including the Popular Front for the Liberation of Palestine (PFLP) and Black September, used skyjacking to win freedom for terrorists imprisoned for earlier terrorist acts, as well as to exact other political concessions. Improvements in security procedures and a growing unwillingness of states to grant political asylum for aircraft hijackers ended the growth in skyjackings after 1979. Another factor was the PLO's realization that hijacking aircraft did little to aid the Palestinian cause.[41]

4. Takeover of Non-Air Transportation—Terrorists gain control of other means of transport, such as trains and ships, and hold the passengers hostage. These operations are uncommon because they are usually difficult to carry out and the propaganda value is typically low. The best-known example was the October 1985 capture of the passenger ship *Achille Lauro* in the Mediterranean Sea. Attempts by the U.S. government to press piracy charges for this act were ignored by the international community.

5. Bombing—The use of an explosive device against a target, either an individual or property, has been a common terrorist weapon. Some of the French and West German terrorist groups used bombings as part of their strategy to destabilize their societies. The IRA-Provos have also launched several bombing campaigns in London and elsewhere in the United Kingdom to bring the war in Northern Ireland home to the British people. Since the mid-1970s, bombing has replaced kidnapping as the

favorite weapon of terrorists. Despite the occasional accident in setting up or delivering the explosives, bombing is one of the safer terrorist tactics. Some terrorists consider bombing counterproductive, however, because it often kills so many bystanders.

6. Letter Bomb—Explosive devices sent through the postal services are used by several terrorist groups. A letter bomb war developed between the Palestinians and the Israelis in the mid-1970s. It was not until the destruction of a letter bomb factory in Lebanon during an Israeli commando operation that this bomb trading ended. Other letter bomb campaigns have been initiated by the IRA-Provos on several occasions. Despite these efforts, casualties from letter bombs have always remained low.[42] Effective monitoring of the mail in most countries has prevented this weapon from becoming more effective.

7. Armed Attack—An armed attack is one that uses heavy weapons in an assault upon a target. Several operations of this type have been planned and started, but terrorist groups have difficulty mobilizing the personnel and heavy weapons necessary to succeed in such an attack. This type of incident has been more common in Central and South America than elsewhere. Only in the last stages of insurgency does this tactic have much chance of success.

8. Murder or Assassination—Assassination is a terrorist tactic to kill a specific individual for political purposes. Because this type of operation is comparatively easy to carry out, it has been attempted frequently. Increased protection for political figures has decreased the success rate of this tactic, but the assassination of Rajiv Gandhi in May 1991 shows that a suicide attack can still be successful.

9. Arson—The use of incendiary devices to set fire to property is a tactic sometimes used by terrorists. Most terrorist groups, however, find arson too unspecific in its targeting to be effective. Arson is also such bad propaganda that terrorist groups tend to look toward other methods.

10. Theft or Break-in—Terrorists use break-ins and robberies as ways to finance their terrorist activities. Robberies are one of the first activities of most terrorist groups because the money can be used to buy weapons and supplies. Robberies have been described as the urban guerrilla's

substitute for a social support system, which rural guerrilla fighters often have, but which urban terrorists may lack, particularly in industrialized states.[43] Most of the Palestinian terrorist groups are able to receive funding from sympathetic states so they do not have to resort to illegal ways to gain financial support. South American terrorists have developed robberies and kidnappings for ransom to finance their terrorist activities almost to an art form.

11. Sabotage—Damage to equipment and facilities by means other than explosives or incendiary devices is resorted to more by sympathizers than the terrorists themselves. This technique has nevertheless been an effective weapon, especially against foreign corporations doing business in Central and South America.

State Terrorism

State terrorism is usually not considered a part of the terrorism debate because this term refers to the domestic use of terror. Police states have traditionally utilized terror as a way to control dissent. Some of the more notorious examples in history have been the use of terror by the revolutionary government of France during 1793–1794, the Nazi government in Germany during 1933–1945, and the Stalin regime in the Soviet Union during 1928–1953. In each case, the state developed an administrative apparatus to control its citizens by a calculated use of fear. Special agents were commissioned by the state to ferret out potential troublemakers. Dissidents, or those designated as potential enemies of the state, either disappeared into concentration camps or were executed. Some scholars insist that the most successful use of terror has been by governments and authorities to create and maintain order.[44] Revolutionary governments have been especially susceptible to using terror to consolidate and protect their new power. Some recent examples have been the Iranian government during 1978–1985, and the Pol Pot regime in Cambodia. It has been claimed that state terrorism has been responsible for a thousand times more victims than international terrorism, but some students of terrorism still refuse to define it as terrorism.[45]

Several countries in Central America and South America have become infamous for their use of police state tactics to impose state terrorism. Argentina is perhaps the best known for its use of terror in the late 1970s and early 1980s. A military junta seized power in 1976, and it utilized the army, police, and death squads to end both terrorist and democratic institutions. So many people disappeared in the counterterrorist crackdown that it is impossible to ascertain the total number murdered.[46] The commission empowered to identify those who disappeared has been able to trace 8,960 people out of about 20,000 individuals who were arrested, but countless others also vanished.[47] It was only the combination of the unsuccessful and costly Falklands War and bad economic conditions that ended the police state in Argentina. Argentina, however, remains a stark example of a state under attack by terrorism resorting to counterterrorist tactics more vicious than those employed by its opponents. Argentinean authorities used secrecy both to provoke fear and as a basis for official deniability.[48]

State terrorism is a controversial subject because it concerns the use of power by the state. The line between policies developed against terrorism and those used by authoritarian regimes is difficult to distinguish. A critic has defined state terrorism in the following ways:[49]

1. A state dominates its own people through fear created by surveillance, disruption of group meetings, control of the news media, beatings, torture, false and mass arrests, false charges and rumors, show trials, killings, summary executions, and capital punishment.
2. The military forces of a state attack targets that put at risk the civilian population residing in another state.
3. A state makes assassination attempts against officials of other states, whether carried out by military strikes, special forces units, or covert operations by "intelligence forces" or their third-party agents.
4. A state engages in covert operations intended to destabilize or subvert another state.[50]

As this list demonstrates, the concept of state terrorism can be extended to conduct by the state that has traditionally not been considered terrorism. In this light, some actions by the U.S. government, such as support for the Nicaraguan Contras in the early 1980s, might be classified as state terrorism. Many nations, and even some of the terrorist groups in Europe and the Middle East, do define U.S. policies in this way.

Technological, Chemical, and Biological Terrorism

The greatest fear among the countries fighting terrorism is that someday the terrorists will gain access to weapons of mass destruction. Terrorists have been able to gain access through arms dealers to many of the modern weapons available to military forces. State-of-the-art weapons, from submachine guns to shoulder-held antiaircraft missiles, have been found in the possession of terrorists. Modern explosives, including C-4 and petaerythrital-tetranitrate (PETN), have also been placed at their disposal. Terrorists also have access to the technology needed to construct a fission-type nuclear device with enough explosive force to destroy a major city. The growth of the international market for plutonium has increased the chances of terrorists gaining possession of plutonium.[51] There is evidence that substantial amounts of weapon-grade uranium and plutonium are missing from U.S. government stockpiles and there has been speculation that some of it may be in terrorist hands.[52] An example is the loss of a quantity of radioactive tritium in the summer of 1989 while it was being moved to a storage area. The tritium could be used in the construction of a small nuclear weapon. An ongoing fear is that terrorists will form an alliance to use a nuclear device to blackmail world governments into major concessions. Another fear is that terrorists will seize a nuclear facility for such a purpose.

Almost as frightening as nuclear terrorism is the threat of chemical and biological terrorism. The U.S. government estimates that between 15 and 30 countries either have chemical weapons or are working to develop them.[53] One of the fears during the 1991 Persian Gulf War was that the Iraqis had access to many chemical and biological weapons and to means for their dispersal. Many terrorist organizations have been able to recruit scientists who can isolate chemicals and viruses to be used as weapons. Biological agents are especially effective antipersonnel weapons because they target human beings and leave property intact.[54] The introduction of these agents into the air or into drinking water would produce heavy casualties.

An accident with airborne anthrax in April 1979 near Sverdlovsk, Soviet Union, killed between 400 and 1,200 people.[55] All states are vulnerable to this type of terrorism. Much of the counterterrorism effort of the United States is directed toward reducing threats of this nature, but no effective military or civilian defense against these agents has been developed.

Terrorism and the Former Soviet Union

The former Soviet Union was long associated with terrorism in the American public mind. Conventional wisdom asserted that terrorism was just one more weapon to be used in a large Soviet arsenal aimed at destabilizing Western society, notwithstanding that Marxist-Leninist theory argues against any association of the class struggle with terrorism,[56] and in fact regards terrorism as counterproductive to class warfare. An exception to this theory was made in the 1960s in the case of wars of national liberation, because in this cause any tactic was seen as justifiable,[57] but Soviet leaders remained consistent in their condemnation of terrorism as counterproductive.[58] Despite these public views, there is much evidence that the KGB encouraged terrorism by training potential terrorists during the 1950s and 1960s. More recently, Soviet weapons were sold or given to terrorist groups. U.S. intelligence efforts to find direct links between the Soviet Union and terrorist organizations were generally unsuccessful, as the relationship was more like that between sponsor and independent client. Soviet aid was never granted unconditionally. The Soviets' conditional support of the Palestinian cause created considerable resentment against them within the PLO leadership.[59]

As the threat of terrorism to the international order increased, Soviet leaders became nervous about possible international and domestic terrorism directed against the Soviet Union. Some of the actions of the more radical terrorist groups caused the Soviets to become less enthusiastic about the foreign policy benefits of terrorism. These feelings came to a head when some of the Palestinian groups in Lebanon designated Soviet diplomats as targets. The death of one of these diplomats caused the Soviet government to make it plain to the terrorists' Arab state sponsors that the Soviet Union would not tolerate any further such activity. By the mid-1970s, Soviet sponsorship of terrorism had lessened, although Soviet equipment was still available to terrorists by way of Soviet client states.

Charges of Soviet complicity in the promotion of international terrorism was always a part of the Cold War debate. Conservatives in the Reagan administration were particularly insistent in condemning Soviet sponsorship of terrorism; however, the administration's experts continued to believe that the Soviets were only guilty of providing financial and military support to countries sponsoring international terrorism.[60] Evidence now indicates that in early 1989 Mikhail Gorbachev began implementing a serious antiterrorism policy, as Soviet leaders feared that the nation was becoming more of a terrorist target.[61] The former Soviet Union and the United States took steps toward resolving terrorist issues with the formation of the U.S.-Soviet Task Force to Prevent Terrorism.[62]

With the radical political changes that caused the breakup of the Soviet Union in 1991, the Commonwealth of Independent States may become more of a restraining agent on terrorist activities than a power pursuing destabilization policies. Still, in a state of political flux, terrorism is always a weapon at hand. Rivalry between the republics and ethnic warfare are both serious problems, but open warfare between the republics is a more serious concern than the widespread use of terrorism.

✳ Terrorism and the Media

Terrorists have always needed publicity to advance their cause. Without publicity, terrorism has little meaning. An adage among terrorists is that bad publicity is better than no publicity. Many terrorist incidents have been staged to provide maximum media coverage. Terrorists consider news as propaganda, and they will do anything to promote publicity. Modern terrorist groups have developed a formula to use the mass media for propaganda, and it is characterized by the following elements:[63]

1. Instill fear in the general population.
2. Polarize public opinion by targeting the powerful and the wealthy.

3. Gain publicity by agreeing to clandestine interviews and demanding publication of a manifesto of their political views.
4. Provoke government overreaction by attacking the military and police.
5. Spread false and misleading information to place opponents on the defensive.
6. Attract converts and support by espousing a popular antigovernment position.
7. Coerce the media by assaulting journalists both physically and verbally.
8. Divert public attention by bombing their way onto the front page.
9. Use the media to excite the public against the government and to send messages to comrades in other countries.
10. Bolster group morale through spectacular terrorist acts.
11. Gain a Robin Hood image by fighting economic and political injustices.
12. Obtain information on counterterrorist strategies and identify future targets.
13. Exploit the media to build an image of the terrorist group as being above the law.

This imposing list shows how important mass media are to a terrorist movement. The importance of the media is such that they are always one of the first targets of a repressive regime's use of terror to control its populace. And relatively few governments allow the media to be critical of their actions. A survey of the UN membership will show that less than 25 percent of the countries have a free press.

Even in more democratic nations, terrorists usually find that the media's response to their actions only bolsters their cause. Acts of terrorism produce big news stories filled with human interest and tragedy. These stories sell newspapers, and television interviews with terrorist participants and victims create larger audiences for news programs. National reputations have been made for journalists and reporters who have covered terrorism; some of them received valuable inside information from terrorists eager for media exposure.

The media have long been criticized by government officials and the public for allowing terrorists to manipulate and use media coverage for terrorist ends. Sometimes over-eager reporters can interfere with hostage negotiations, and the consequences can be tragic.[64]

Elements in the U.S. government have placed severe pressure on the journalism profession to act responsibly. Because of such efforts, the American public was sometimes unaware of the nature or the extent of terrorist activity in the late 1980s and early 1990s. Only a few newspapers, such as the *New York Times* and the *Washington Post,* cover terrorism regularly.

The media have also been used by government authorities for political reasons. For example, on occasion the government gives the media misinformation about the threat of terrorism. A Central Intelligence Agency (CIA) tale about a Libyan assassination team operating in the United States in the early 1980s was one such false information plant.[65] This type of incident has muddled the relationship between the government and the media in their reporting of terrorism.

Counterterrorism

Each state responds differently to terrorism, but the record shows that the Western democratic states have had the greatest difficulty adjusting to it. Warfare against unsuspecting citizens in a time of peace has always been difficult for the general public to accept. Moreover, terrorism operates most efficiently in democratic societies with their variety of constitutional guarantees. Terrorists are not above using these guarantees as weapons against these states.

Different states develop a variety of options in dealing with terrorism. These include policies of compliance, negotiation, compromise, and retaliation.[66]

Compliance is used by those states that sympathize with the aims of the terrorists. For example, most of the Middle East states support the Palestinian cause. In a terrorist incident involving the PLO or the PFLP, these states give moral and physical help. Hijacked aircraft are allowed to land, the hijackers surrender, and they are given over to a sympathetic hand. Only rarely are any of these terrorists punished. Often the terrorists reappear on the international scene in another terrorist act months or years later. Libya is the most obvious of the compliance states, but Algeria, Iraq, Syria, and Kuwait have also engaged in this type of behavior. Compliance and sponsorship are regarded as almost identical strategies among the Western states.

Through negotiation, states deal with terrorist demands directly, hoping that by cooperating with the terrorists they will avoid future terrorist activity on their soil. The French government has characterized this policy as one of "strict neutrality."[67] Greece also pursued this policy, but both countries encountered trouble at home and from their allies because of it. France began to reconsider this policy in the early 1980s because its nearly open-door policy toward terrorism caused Paris to become one of the centers of terrorist activity on the European continent. Greece has seen its profitable tourist industry seriously damaged by tourism boycotts because of its perceived tolerance toward terrorism.

Compromise is a technique used by states that grudgingly give concessions to terrorists to end a specific terrorist act. Most often this compromise is in the form of guaranteed safe passage for the terrorists in exchange for the release of hostages. Sometimes the compromise takes the form of release of imprisoned terrorists, or the paying of a ransom. Every state has engaged in compromise at one time or another, because even communicating with terrorists in a kidnapping or hostage-taking is part of a compromise strategy.

Only a few states pursue a policy of retaliation against terrorism, and they back down in special circumstances. This policy means that no concessions are made during a terrorist incident, and force is used against the terrorists at the earliest point possible. In the event that force is inappropriate during the terrorist act, the state then retaliates against the responsible terrorist organization. A problem always arises in identifying the offending terrorist organization and finding the means to retaliate against it. Israel has been the most active practitioner of the retaliatory response, but some evidence suggests that this hardline policy has served as a challenge to Palestinian terrorists to escalate their attacks.[68] Israeli retaliation appears to have provoked an endless spiral of stroke and counterstroke between Israel and the Palestinians. Preemptive strikes against terrorist targets are also part of Israeli policy, and this too has spurred further Palestinian attacks.

Both the former Soviet Union and the United States have subscribed to this nonnegotiation and retaliation strategy. The National Security Decision Directive 138 of April 1984 made legal the use of retaliatory military force against terrorists who attack U.S. interests. Subsequent use of this authority in an attack by U.S. military forces against Libya in April 1986, however, showed the limits of the strategy. World opinion was so hostile to the destruction and the civilian deaths from that attack that it is unlikely that this type of action will be used again. Moreover, both the United States and the former Soviet Union have had to back down in situations where retaliation was deemed inappropriate. While the Soviet Union found that state control and a no-concessions policy made terrorism unattractive inside the former Soviet Union, this policy was unworkable outside Soviet borders.[69]

Every state has built some type of counterterrorism capability, and the Western states have devoted considerable resources to develop it. New counterterrorism forces have been formed and legislation has been passed to help these forces operate effectively against terrorism. Examples are the passage by the British Parliament of the Prevention of Terrorism Act of 1974, which was promulgated to combat the IRA, and the U.S. Congress' passage of the Comprehensive Crime Control Act of 1984, which was intended to close legal loopholes that might allow terrorists to escape detection and arrest. Cooperation between police forces in Western Europe and the United States has helped the flow of information about terrorist organizations and personnel. Well-trained, elite military units and police SWAT teams have been formed to handle emergency situations. Fiascos, such as the ill-fated West German police attempt to rescue hostages in Munich in 1972, proved the need for such units. Even such relatively small-scale efforts as increased airport security have produced dividends: aircraft hijacking now occurs only rarely. Many of these procedures have been time-consuming and expensive, but most travelers understand that inconvenience is a small price to pay to avoid aircraft hijackings.

Incentives offered to terrorists to abandon their actions or to subvert their own organizations have met with some success. The Italian government's agreements with the Red Brigade showed that offers of reduced prison sentences were a powerful inducement for captured terrorists to provide information about other members.[70] The most successful approach, however, is the offer of rewards for information.[71] Large rewards are always a threat to the safety of terrorists and every effort is made by terrorist groups to make examples of informers.

Successes notwithstanding, counterterrorism policies always have some dangers. Excessive or misdirected policies can rebound negatively. Three lessons have been identified in dealing with terrorism:[72]

1. A policy of massive retaliation against terrorists, their suppliers, and their sympathizers is a war policy with all the dangers of warmaking.

2. Terrorism alone virtually never accomplishes the task of igniting a general conflagration, but it may prepare the way for one.

3. To conceive of terrorism as the mere product of outside manipulation, created by the machinations of this government or that, makes it impossible to understand either its causes or its consequences.

Consequently, counterterrorism combines the dangers of over-reaction to individual incidents, misunderstanding of the nature of terrorism, and overestimation of the capabilities of the terrorists. Some evidence exists that U.S. counterterrorism policy may have reached these limits. A manual prepared by the CIA and entitled *Psychological Operations in Guerrilla Wars* (a Spanish version appeared in October 1984) advocates "neutralization" of selected individuals in a coordinated counterterrorism campaign.[73] According to the manual, these assassinations of key personnel would rid the guerrilla-terrorists of financial and moral support by terrorizing their potential backers. This sort of counterterrorism resembles the tactics of the terrorists themselves, and makes it difficult for outsiders to distinguish the good guys from the bad guys.

Political Hostages

Political hostage-taking has been one of the most effective techniques used by terrorists. Most often hostages have been taken during aircraft hijackings, but trains and ships have been seized to gain hostages. Urban terrorists have conducted kidnappings of prominent officials in busy urban thoroughfare ambushes.[74] The hostage situation in Iran during 1979–1980 proved to terrorists that the taking of large numbers of hostages could bring about concessions even from the super-powers. Many other instances of hostage-taking have produced media attention, the release of colleagues being held as political prisoners, and even financial benefits.

These benefits have become so important to the terrorists that they depend on hostage incidents as a primary weapon to gain concessions. The key to resolving hostage scenarios is the negotiations between the government and the terrorists.[75] They must find terms for trade, or else nothing can be accomplished to resolve the situation.[76] Experts have concluded that a successful hostage negotiation has three phases: a realistic diagnosis of the situation, the discovery of a mutually acceptable formula to frame the agreement, and a way of implementing the formula with an agreement on details.[77] Attempts to proceed without these phases means that the negotiations will probably fail.

Enough evidence has accumulated about the psychology of hostage-taking that hostage experts can now count on certain constants. One pattern is that "the longer the hostage-taking incident continues, the greater the probability the hostages will be released unharmed."[78] Time also allows the psychological process called the Stockholm Syndrome to manifest itself. The Stockholm Syndrome, or Hostage Identification Syndrome (HIS), is an identification by the hostage with the hostage-taker and a growing sympathy of the hostage-taker with the hostage. It may manifest itself in the following ways:[79]

1. Positive feelings of the hostages toward the hostage-takers.
2. Reciprocal, positive feelings of the hostage-takers toward the hostages.
3. Negative feelings of both the hostages and hostage-takers toward the police and the government.

Studies of this syndrome indicate that face-to-face contact and verbal communication of some form are critical elements necessary for the syndrome to develop.[80] This type of interaction explains the conversion of Patty Hearst to the cause of the Symbionese Liberation Army and her acceptance by the terrorists. Evidence is available that some of the Palestinian terrorist groups train their members against the Stockholm Syndrome.[81] Police negotiators can promote the acceleration of these feelings between the hostage-taker and the hostage by allowing time for them to develop and by asking about the health of the hostages.

Kidnapping is a form of hostage-taking except that it usually involves only one person, typically a prominent politician or businessman. Terrorist motivation for a kidnapping can usually be traced to one or more of four reasons:[82]

1. To release imprisoned terrorists.
2. To publicize terrorist objectives.
3. To humiliate the national government.

4. To change established social, political, or economic programs.

Evidence is lacking on the full effect of the Stockholm Syndrome on kidnappings, but the syndrome seems to operate only if both sides let it happen.

Hostage-taking continues to be popular among terrorist groups. Terrorists in Lebanon seized numerous hostages and used them to manipulate public opinion among the Western democracies. These terrorists, however, have learned the limitations of this tactic. Hostages have an impact only if Western public opinion can be mobilized. If results do not occur quickly, terrorists must expend resources in setting up multiple safe houses to thwart rescue attempts, ensure medical care, provide food, and assign personnel the task of guarding the hostages.

Hostage-taking of businessmen operates under a different set of rules than do political kidnappings. Western governments have developed a calculated policy of not attempting rescue of hostages. They have learned the hard way that rescue attempts rarely succeed, and they refuse to allow terrorists to blackmail them into concessions. Corporations have a different perspective: save the life of the hostage at all costs.[83] These corporations are willing to pay ransom to terrorists for the release of a hostage, even when governments are unwilling to go along. Because the lengthy ransom negotiations are often held outside the knowledge of law enforcement agencies, most business hostage negotiations are never publicized. Terrorists have been able to finance other activities with the funds raised through this kind of kidnapping. An example is the 1975 kidnapping of two Argentinian grain dealers by the Montoneros. The captives were released after nine months with the payment of $60 million in ransom. A portion of the money was distributed to the poor in the form of food and money.

Legal Responses to Terrorism

The international community realized by the early 1970s that new legal steps were necessary to control terrorism. Members of the UN, however, have been so divided over defining and identifying terrorism that no legal agreements on terrorism have been possible. So few member states even ratified the 1973 Agreement on the Protection of Diplomats that it is not yet in force. Declarations and conventions from the UN have lacked effective enforcement mechanisms, so they have been ignored by member states and have been characterized as "largely cosmetic."[84]

Efforts by regional organizations have also been slow to coalesce around antiterrorism policies. One example is the leisurely pace taken in adopting the recommendations of the Council of Europe's European Convention on the Suppression of Terrorism (ECST). These recommendations were agreed upon by the representatives of the Council of Europe in 1973, but it took more than a decade for the European Community members to bridge political and legal differences to produce a common policy for combatting terrorism in Europe. Extradition for terrorist crimes has been the most divisive issue.[85] Only in the mid-1980s was a common policy adopted by member states.

Bilateral agreements between states have proved more useful than either UN or regional efforts. An agreement between the United States and Cuba in 1973 ended the steady stream of aircraft hijackings between them. Other agreements have been slower to be concluded because some countries, especially those in Central and South America, refuse to limit the right of political asylum.[86] Even European countries have been reluctant to adopt antiterrorism measures. France, in particular, has created obstacles against tough policies. French authorities were reluctant to change the French tradition of accepting refugees charged with political crimes. It was not until the early 1980s that some European agreements on controlling terrorism began to take effect. The *Achille Lauro* terrorist incident in 1985 showed, however, that divergent political interests come into play in any terrorist event. Egypt, Italy, and the United States each allowed international and domestic political considerations to outweigh agreements and treaties among them. If the political stakes are high enough, states may ignore antiterrorist agreements.

When terrorist activity heated up in the 1960s, most countries tried to fight it with traditional police methods. Police authorities soon found that they lacked the enforcement techniques and the legal authority to suppress even weak terrorist organizations. Part of the problem was the tendency by virtually all governments to deny that political crimes are distinct from common criminal acts.[87] Only with the growing awareness that terrorism demands different legal instruments were governments able to begin bringing terrorism under control. Italy was only able to overcome the Red Brigade terrorist campaign by instituting the toughest antiterrorist legislation in Europe. Italian police are allowed warrantless searches and wiretaps, detention of suspects for 48 hours without notification, and detainment of terrorists for up to 12 years without trial. Even Great Britain and West Germany have reduced constitutional rights in an effort to fight terrorism. Some South American states, such as Argentina, Chile, and Uruguay, have instituted so many legal restrictions that they have imposed state terrorism to fight revolutionary terrorism. Somewhere there lies a happy medium between controlling terrorism by legal means and preserving democratic institutions. Unhappily, only a few states have been able to reconcile the two approaches.

Notes

1. Richard E. Rubenstein, *Alchemists of Revolution: Terrorism in the Modern World* (New York: Basic Books, 1987), 7–8.

2. William D. Perdue, *Terrorism and the State: A Critique of Domination through Fear* (New York: Praeger, 1989), 3.

3. James Lodge, *Terrorism: A Challenge to the State* (Oxford: Martin Robertson, 1981), 5.

4. Thomas P. Thornton, "Terror as a Weapon of Political Agitation," in *Internal War*, ed. H. Eckstein (New York: Free Press, 1964), 71–99.

5. Robert A. Friedlander, *Terrorism and the Law: What Price Safety?* (Gaithersburg, MD: IACP, 1981), 3.

6. Lester A. Sobel, *Political Terrorism* (New York: Facts on File, 1975), 3–12.

7. James Poland, *Understanding Terrorism: Groups, Strategies, and Responses* (Englewood Cliffs, NJ: Prentice Hall, 1988), 11.

8. Antonio Cassesse, *Terrorism, Politics and Law: The Achille Lauro Affair* (Princeton, NJ: Princeton University Press, 1989), 6.

9. Rubenstein, xvi.

10. Juliet Lodge, ed., *The Threat of Terrorism* (Boulder, CO: Westview, 1988), xii.

11. Martha Crenshaw, "Theories of Terrorism: Instrumental and Organizational Approaches," in *Inside Terrorist Organizations*, ed. David C. Rapoport (New York: Columbia University Press, 1988), 14–15.

12. Donald J. Hanle, *Terrorism: The Newest Face of Warfare* (Washington, DC: Pergamon-Brassey's International Defense Publishers, 1989), 235–239.

13. Maxwell Taylor, *The Terrorist* (London: Brassey's Defence Publishers, 1988), 6.

14. Paul Wilkinson, *Terrorism and the Liberal State*, 2d ed. (London: Macmillan, 1986), 51.

15. Ibid.

16. Ibid., 54.

17. Ibid., 55.

18. Ibid.

19. Ibid.

20. Ibid., 55–56.

21. Brian Jenkins, *International Terrorism: A New Mode of Conflict* (Los Angeles: Crescent, 1975), 4–7.

22. Christopher Seton-Watson, "Terrorism in Italy,"in *The Threat of Terrorism*, ed. Juliet Lodge (Boulder, CO: Westview, 1988), 92.

23. Rubenstein, 127.

24. Ibid., 128.

25. Walter Laqueur, *The Age of Terrorism* (Boston: Little, Brown, 1987), 139.

26. Rubenstein, 197–198.

27. "Patterns of Global Terrorism: 1987," in *Terrorism: Documents of International and Local Control*, ed. Robert A. Friedlander (London: Oceana, 1990), 4:168–171.

28. Grant Wardlaw, "Terror as an Instrument of Foreign Policy," in *Inside Terrorist Organizations*, ed. David C. Rapoport (New York: Columbia University Press, 1988), 238–239.

29. Cassesse, 11–12.

30. James Adams, *The Financing of Terror: How the Groups That Are Terrorizing the World Get the Money to Do It* (New York: Simon & Schuster, 1986), 64.

31. Ibid., 112. Adams estimates that the PLO has control of around $2 billion in assets, and, if all the different groups in the PLO are counted, it has as much as $5 billion in assets (p. 109).

32. Crenshaw, 28.

33. Wardlaw, 243–244.

34. Albert O. Hirschman, *Exit, Voice, and Loyalty: Responses to Decline in Firms, Organizations, and States* (Cambridge, MA: Harvard University Press, 1970), 121.

35. Ibid.

36. Laqueur, 95.

37. P. N. Grabosky, "The Urban Context of Political Terrorism," in *The Politics of Terrorism*, ed. Michael Stohl (New York: Marcel Dekker, 1979), 58-59.

38. Albert Parry, *Terrorism: From Robespierre to Arafat* (New York: Vanguard, 1976), 12.

39. The following general types of incidents have been taken from an analysis by Edward Mickolus in "Transnational Terrorism," in *The Politics of Terrorism*, ed. Michael Stohl, (New York: Marcel Dekker, 1979), 150.

40. Ibid., 152.

41. Taylor, 30.

42. Vaughn F. Bishop, "The Role of Political Terrorism in the Palestinian Resistance Movement: June 1967–October 1973" in *The Politics of Terrorism*, ed. Michael Stohl. (New York: Marcel Dekker, 1979), 343.

43. Eva Kolinsky, "Terrorism in West Germany," in *The Threat of Terrorism*, ed. Juliet Lodge (Boulder, CO: Westview, 1988), 63.

44. Michael Stohl, "Introduction: Myths and Realities of Political Terrorism" in *The Politics of Terrorism*, ed. Michael Stohl (New York: Marcel Dekker, 1979), 4.

45. The most prominent scholar has been Walter Laqueur, who maintains that besides their aim of inducing a state of fear among the enemy there are no similarities between state and individual substate terrorism. See Laqueur, 146.

46. Taylor uses the figures 20,000 arrested, 11,000 disappeared, and 2 million fleeing the country between 1976 and 1983, but nobody will ever know the exact toll. See Taylor, 44.

47. Michael Simpson and Jana Bennett, *The Disappeared and the Mothers of the Plaza: The Story of the 11,000 Argentineans Who Vanished* (New York: St. Martin's, 1985), 7.

48. Grabosky, 62.

49. Perdue, 42.

50. Perdue has a further list, but these four give the essence of his interpretation of state terrorism. See Perdue, 42–43.

51. Robert Kupperman and Jeff Kamen, *Final Warning: Averting Disaster in the New Age of Terrorism* (New York: Doubleday, 1989), 97.

52. Poland, 197.

53. Kupperman and Kamen, 100.

54. Stanley Wiener, "Chemical and Biological Weapons and Terrorism," in *International Terrorism: Policy Implications,* ed. Susan Flood (Chicago: University of Illinois at Chicago, Office of International Criminal Justice, 1991), 65.

55. Ibid, 66–67.

56. A concise treatment of the antiterrorism theory of Marxism-Leninism is given in Rubenstein, 43–45.

57. Galia Golan, *Gorbachev's "New Thinking"on Terrorism.* (New York: Praeger, 1990), 7–10.

58. Ibid., 17–18.

59. Adams, 44.

60. Wardlaw, 237–238.

61. Kupperman and Kamen, 16.

62. Igor Beliaev and John Marks, eds., *Common Ground on Terrorism: Soviet-American Cooperation Against the Politics of Terror* (New York: Norton, 1991), 20–22.

63. Alex P. Schmid and Janny de Graaf, *Violence as Communication: Insurgent Terrorism and the Western News Media* (Newbury Park, CA: Sage, 1982), 53–54.

64. Poland, 61–62.

65. Perdue, 52–54.

66. Stephen Segaller, *Invisible Armies: Terrorism into the 1990s* (San Diego: Harcourt Brace Jovanovich, 1987), 178.

67. Michel Wieviorka, "French Politics and Strategy on Terrorism," in *The Politics of Counterterrorism: The Ordeal of Democratic States,* ed. Barry Rubin (Washington, DC: Johns Hopkins Foreign Policy Institute, 1990), 68–69.

68. Stohl, 7.

69. Segaller, 152.

70. Crenshaw, 25.

71. Laqueur, 127–129.

72. These lessons have been borrowed with some minor changes from Rubenstein, xviii–xix.

73. Adams, 20–21.

74. Grabosky, 63.

75. I. William Zartman, "Negotiating Effectively with Terrorists" in *The Politics of Counterterrorism: The Ordeal of Democratic States,* ed. Barry Rubin (Washington, DC: Johns Hopkins Foreign Policy Institute, 1990), 169–171.

76. Ibid., 174–175.

77. Ibid., p.171.

78. Poland, p. 129.

79. Murray S. Miron and Arnold P. Goldstein, *Hostage* (New York: Pergamon, 1979), 9.

80. Taylor, 21.

81. Poland, 131.

82. Ibid., 137.

83. Robert Glendon, "International Terrorism and Business" in *International Terrorism: Policy Implications* (Chicago: University of Illinois at Chicago, Office of International Criminal Justice, 1991), 32–33.

84. Robert A. Friedlander, *Terrorism: Documents of International and Local Control* (London: Oceana, 1981), 3: 12.

85. Juliet Lodge, "Introduction—Terrorism and Europe: Some General Considerations," in *The Threat of Terrorism,* ed. Juliet Lodge (Boulder, CO: Westview, 1988), 18–19.

86. Mickolus, 180.

87. Stohl, 7.

2

Selected Chronology of Terrorist Events, 1894–1992

A CHRONOLOGY IS ESSENTIAL IN ILLUSTRATING the patterns of behavior of terrorist groups. Terrorism has evolved in a particular way, with new groups forming and adopting new strategies and tactics. Sometimes a splinter group will emerge from a larger terrorist organization, and the only means of tracing this evolution is through examining the terrorist acts themselves. Often a terrorist organization will test a new tactic in a specific incident to gauge its effectiveness before launching a full-scale campaign. Several terrorist groups will often claim responsibility for the same assassination or bombing.

A chronology allows the reader to follow the ebb and flow of terrorism and to note the changing of the actors. This listing reflects only a small portion of the terrorist incidents during the last century. It is impossible to be exact on the number of terrorist acts during this timespan, but the best estimates suggest that they have numbered in the hundreds of thousands. Factual information on the incidents are sometimes difficult to obtain. Court trials and newspaper reports are the best sources, but certain information never makes it into print. The following chronology shows dates and brief descriptions of major terrorist incidents during 1894–1992. For more information about the organizations and individuals cited in the chronology, please see the Biographical Profiles and Directory of Terrorist Organizations sections.

Chronology of Terrorism

1894   June 24. French President Sadi Carnot assassinated by an Italian anarchist in Lyons.

1914   June 28. Austria's Archduke Francis Ferdinand and his wife assassinated by Gavrilo Princip and the Serbian Union or Death Group in Sarajevo. This act starts events resulting in World War I.

1931   February 21. First skyjacking of aircraft, an F7 Ford Trimotor, in Peru.

1934   October 9. King Alexander of Yugoslavia and the French Foreign Minister shot by a Croatian member of the Iron Hand terrorist group. This assassination causes an international incident, and the League of Nations passes two conventions in 1937 to try to control international terrorism. Few nations ratify the conventions so this attempt to deal with terrorism fails.

1936–1939   Arab terrorism against British military and Jewish population in Palestine.

1939–1992   Irish Republican Army (IRA) terrorist campaign in United Kingdom for independence of Northern Ireland.

1944–1948   Jewish terrorism against British forces in Palestine.

1944   November 6. Members of the Jewish Terrorist Stern Gang assassinate the former British colonial secretary, Lord Moyne, in Cairo, Egypt.

1946   July 22. Members of the Jewish terrorist group Irgun Zvai Leumi blow up the King David Hotel in Jerusalem, killing 91 and wounding 45. This terrorist act brings universal condemnation.

1947   July 12. Two British army sergeants, Clifford Martin and Mervyn Paice, kidnapped by the Jewish terrorist group Irgun in Natanya and held as hostages for four condemned Irgun members. The sergeants are hanged on July 30 in retaliation for the execution of the Irgun members.

1948   February 22. Arab terrorists bomb armored trucks with explosives on Ben Yahuda Street in Jerusalem, resulting in 54 deaths.

February 29. Jewish terrorists of the Stern Gang blow up the Cairo-Haifa train in retaliation for the Ben Yehuda Street incident, causing the deaths of 28 British soldiers and injuring another 35.

September 17. Members of the Jewish terrorist Stern Gang assassinate UN mediator Count Folke Bernadotte.

1950–   A number of aircraft are hijacked in Communist countries in
1953   Eastern Europe, and political asylum is granted to most of the anti-Communist hijackers.

1950   November 1. Two Puerto Rican nationalists attempt to assassinate President Harry S. Truman in Washington, DC.

1951   July 20. Jordan's King Abdulla Ibn Hussein killed in Jerusalem by a member of the Palestinian terrorist group Jihad Mukadess. This assassination discourages Arab states from negotiating with the new state of Israel.

1954   March 1. Four Puerto Rican nationalists wound five U.S. congressmen.

1955–   Under the leadership of General George Grivas, the Ethniki
1958   Organosis Kyprion Agoniston (EOKA) carries out terrorist campaigns to unite Cyprus with Greece beginning in March 1955 with a wave of bombings.

1955–   Algerian terrorists conduct an open war against French forces
1960   and civilians in Algeria. The guerrilla-terrorist organization the National Liberation Front (FLN), wins the war and Algeria is granted independence from France.

1956   May 9. Three British soldiers and four Greek Cypriots are killed in Ktima, Cyprus, by Cypriot terrorists of EOKA in protest of the scheduled execution of two terrorists.

1958   June 27. Cuban insurgents of the Twenty-Sixth of July Movement hold 30 U.S. Marine Corps personnel hostage, releasing them in stages during mid-July.

September 15. Three Algerian terrorists unsuccessfully attempt to assassinate the French Information Minister, Jacques Soustelle, in Paris.

1958–   A terrorist campaign is executed by Fidel Castro and the
1959   Twenty-Sixth of July Movement in order to overthrow the Batista government.

1959–   Various anti-Castro Cuban terrorist groups conduct operations
1965   against Castro Cuba. Most of the aircraft hijackers given political asylum in the United States.

1961–   Efforts by the French terrorist group, OAS, to retain Algeria as a
1965   French colony and to assassinate the French President, Charles de Gaulle, for his granting of independence to Algeria.

1963   November 22. President John F. Kennedy assassinated in Dallas, Texas, allegedly by Lee Harvey Oswald. Several inquiries have been held to determine the participants in this assassination, but a conspiracy has never been proven. Because Kennedy's assassination was an act to change the political course of the United States, it is classified as a terrorist action.

1964   December 31. First recorded terrorist act against Israel by a Palestinian terrorist group.

1965–   Movement for National Liberation (Tupamaros) conducts
1971   terrorist activities in Uruguay.

1965   February 16. A plot to blow up the Liberty Bell, Statue of Liberty, and Washington Monument foiled by police and FBI.

1968   January 16. Terrorists in Guatemala kill Colonel John D. Webber and Lieutenant Commander Ernest A. Munro and wound two other American soldiers. Although no group claimed responsibility, radical elements of the Rebel Armed Forces (FAR) probably carried out this operation to highlight their opposition to U.S. policies in Central America.

1968
cont.

April 4. Civil rights leader Martin Luther King, Jr., assassinated in Memphis, Tennessee. A suspect, James Earl Ray, arrested and sentenced to life imprisonment. This terrorist act removed the most powerful figure in the civil rights movement and radicalized the movement further.

July 22. Presidential candidate Senator Robert F. Kennedy killed by a Jordanian nationalist, Sirhan Sirhan. He is sentenced to life in a federal prison. While no evidence has appeared about a conspiracy, Kennedy's assassination was intended to protest Kennedy's support of Israel.

July 22. Three members of the Popular Front for the Liberation of Palestine (PFLP) hijack an El Al Boeing 707 on its way from Rome to Tel Aviv, creating an international incident when the Algerian government aids the hijackers in attaining their demands.

August 28. U.S. Ambassador to Guatemala, John Gordon Mein, assassinated by terrorists in Guatemala City, Guatemala. Members of the Rebel Armed Forces carried out this operation.

1969

August 29. TWA Flight 840 hijacked outside of Rome by members of PFLP. First appearance of the terrorist Leila Ali Khaled. All passengers released in Damascus, Syria, except for six Israeli citizens who are held hostage until Israel agrees to release 71 Arab prisoners. This exchange is the last hostage arrangement of this type that Israel has participated in.

September 4. Charles Burke Elbrick, U.S. Ambassador to Brazil, kidnapped in Rio de Janeiro. Police rescue him from his kidnappers, but only after 15 Brazilian political prisoners are released and granted political asylum in Mexico.

November 4. Carlos Marighella, a leader of the Acao Libertadora Nacional (ALN), is killed in a police ambush in São Paulo, Brazil.

1970

February 21. Swiss Air Flight 330 crashes after a bomb explodes in the rear luggage compartment, killing 38 people. A representative of the PFLP at first claims responsibility, but, after a public outcry over the bombing, withdraws the claim.

March 31. Nine members of the Japanese Red Army (JRA) hijack a Japan Air Lines B727 after takeoff from Tokyo.

1970
cont.   After an attempt to fool the hijackers by a fake landing in Seoul, South Korea, the plane is flown to Pyongyang, North Korea. Hostages are released by the North Korean government.

March 31. West German Ambassador Count Karl von Spreti kidnapped in Guatemala City by the Rebel Armed Forces. Unlike its response to other kidnapping cases, the Guatemalan government refuses to release the 17 political prisoners demanded by the kidnappers. Despite some steps by the West German government to intervene, the demands are ignored and the kidnappers murder the ambassador on April 4.

June 9. Members of the PFLP seize two Amman, Jordan, hotels, the Philadelphia and the Intercontinental, and 60 foreign hostages. They demand the dismissal of the army commander-in-chief and his replacement by a pro-Palestinian general. After a three-day siege, King Hussein agrees to the demands and the hostages are freed.

June 11. Members of the Juarez Guimarez de Brito command of the ALN and VPR kidnap West German Ambassador Ehrenfried von Holleben in Rio de Janeiro, Brazil. Demands made for the release of 40 political prisoners. After these demands are met and the prisoners land in Algeria, the ambassador is released.

July 31. Tupamaros guerrillas kidnap Daniel A. Mitrione, an American police official and advisor to the Uruguayan government, and kill him after the Uruguayan government refuses to meet the kidnappers' demands. Antonio Mas Mas was charged with his murder and sentenced to 30 years in jail in 1977.

September 6. A series of aircraft hijackings conducted by members of the PFLP. Two of the planes are flown to Amman, Jordan. After lengthy negotiations, the Jordanian armed forces clash with the Palestinians in a series of battles, in which approximately 7,000 PFLP supporters are killed. Hostages from the planes freed unharmed at various Palestinian refugee camps. Terrorists dub this attack Black September.

October 5. The Quebec Liberation Front (FLQ) kidnaps the British trade commissioner in Quebec, James Richard Jasper Cross; five days later they also kidnap the Quebec minister of labor, Pierre Laporte. Canadian police launch a massive search, and the body of Laporte is found on 18 October.

1970
cont.
After Cross's kidnappers release him on December 3, seven members of the FLQ are flown to Cuba under part of the exchange agreement.

1971
January 8. The British ambassador to Uruguay, Sir Geoffrey M. S. Jackson, kidnapped in Montevideo by 20 Tupamaros terrorists. On 8 September, two days after 106 Tupamaros escaped from jail, they release him.

March 1. A bomb explodes in a men's lavatory in the Senate wing of the U.S. Capitol, resulting in considerable damage but no injuries. The Weather Underground claims responsibility for the bombing.

April 7. Two Croatian terrorists assassinate the Yugoslavian Ambassador to Sweden, Vladimir Rolovic. The terrorists are arrested and sentenced to life imprisonment.

May 17. Four members of the Turkish Revolutionary Youth Federation (TRYF) kidnap and murder the Israeli Consul General in Istanbul. Over the next several months, a massive crackdown on terrorist groups by the Turkish government results in the deaths or arrests of all of the kidnappers.

November 28. Members of Black September terrorist group assassinate Jordanian Prime Minister Wasfi el-Tal in Cairo, Egypt. The terrorists are captured, but heavy Arab pressure, especially from Libya, causes Egypt to free the assassins. This assassination is in retaliation for the crackdown on Palestinians by Jordanian authorities.

1972
February 22. Members of the Irish Republican Army (IRA) plant a car bomb in front of the kitchen of the Aldershot Army Base near London. Nine people die and seventeen are wounded. Several IRA members are arrested and an explosives expert is sentenced to life imprisonment.

May 8. Sabrena Airlines Flight 517 hijacked over Zagreb, Yugoslavia, by four members of the Black September terrorist group. The plane is redirected to Lod Airport in Israel. The terrorists demand the release of 317 Palestinian prisoners held by the Israelis. Israeli forces, led by Defense Minister Moshe Dayan, assault the aircraft and free the hostages.

1972 One hostage dies and four are wounded; two of the hijackers
cont. are killed during the assault, and the other two sentenced to life
imprisonment.

May 11. Members of the Red Army Faction of West Germany
bomb the Frankfurt headquarters of the 5th U.S. Army Corps.
Colonel Paul Bloomquist killed and 13 others wounded. The
bombing is supposedly in retaliation for U.S. actions against
North Vietnam. Three members of the group sentenced to life
imprisonment in 1977 for the bombing.

May 24. Two bombs in parked cars at U.S. Army-Europe
headquarters in Heidelberg, West Germany, kill three American
soldiers and wound five others. The Red Army Faction claims
responsibility. Leaders of this group captured in June are held
for three years before a 23-month trial. Andreas Baader, Gudrun
Ensslin, and Jan-Carl Raspe were sentenced to life plus 15 years.

May 30. Three members of the Japanese Red Army (JRA) assault
passengers arriving on an Air France flight at the Lod Airport,
Israel, with small arms fire. They kill 28 passengers and wound
76. Two of the three gunmen, on loan from the PFLP, are also
killed, and the survivor captured and sentenced to life
imprisonment.

July 8. Ghassan Kanafani, editor of the PFLP's weekly journal *Al
Hadef,* and his niece are killed when a bomb explodes in his car.
Kanafani had been implicated in the attack on the Lod Airport
and the PFLP charges that Israeli agents planted the bomb in
his car.

July 31. Five Black Panther Party members hijack a Delta DC8
over Florida. They demand and receive a $1 million ransom and
a flight to Algeria. The passengers are freed in Miami, and the
hijackers flown to Algiers. Most of the hijackers are arrested in
Paris in 1976 and placed on trial in France on hijacking charges.

August 15. Argentinian political escapees hijack an Austral
BAC111 at Trelew, Argentina, ordering the plane flown to
Santiago, Chile. The hijackers are among 26 political prisoners
who had escaped during a mutiny at an army maximum security
prison at Rawson, Argentina. They are granted political asylum
by President Allende before being allowed to fly to Cuba on
August 25. Other escapees are captured, and most of them
killed a week later in an alleged prison escape.

1972
cont.

September 5. Eight members of the Black September terrorist group break into the Israeli quarters at the Olympic Games in Munich, West Germany, killing two athletes and taking nine others hostage. They demand the release of 236 guerrillas in Israeli prisons and selected other terrorists in West German prisons. The hostages are killed along with five of the terrorists in a gun battle with police. Three of the terrorists survive and are captured, though another hijacking in October 1972 results in their release. Israelis retaliate for the attack by raiding refugee camps in Lebanon on February 21, 1973. Some evidence exists that the Israelis formed assassination squads to kill the leaders of the Olympics attack.

December 28. Four members of Black September occupy the Israeli embassy in Bangkok, Thailand, threatening to blow it up unless 36 terrorists held in Israeli prisons are released. Thai officials persuade them to release their hostages in exchange for safe passage out of the country. The leadership of Black September criticizes its followers for backing down.

1973

March 1. Eight members of Black September seize the Saudi Arabian embassy in Khartoum, Sudan, demanding the freedom of a number of Palestinian terrorists held in Israel. Two American diplomats and one Belgian diplomat are killed after the demands are not met. The terrorists are sentenced to lengthy prison terms, but the President of Sudan turns the prisoners over to the PLO in Egypt.

April 10. In a series of raids, Israeli commandos attack the headquarters of Black September in Beirut, Lebanon, killing 17 terrorists and destroying a letter bomb factory.

May 4. Members of the People's Revolutionary Armed Forces kidnap U.S. Consul General Terence G. Leonhardy in Guadalajara, Mexico. They demand the release of 30 prisoners in Mexican prisons and a plane to fly them to Cuba.

The Mexican government complies with the terms, and the family of the victim pays $80,000 to the kidnappers. Leonhardy released on May 6.

August 5. Two members of the National Arab Youth for the Liberation of Palestine (NAYLP) assault passengers in the Athens Airport, killing 3 and wounding 55.

1973
cont.
The terrorists then seize 35 hostages, but, after brief negotiations, surrender to the Athens police. Although the terrorists are sentenced to death by a Greek court, the Greek government expels them to Libya in May 1974.

September 28. Two members of the Thunderbolt (al-Sa'iga) Palestinian terrorist group seize a passenger train in Austria, demanding that Austria close down the Schonau Castle facility for Soviet Jewish émigrés. They also want the end of further émigré movement to Israel through Austria. The terrorists are permitted to leave Austria, and the Schonau Castle facility is shut down. While Soviet Jews are allowed to use other facilities in transit, the Austrian Prime Minister, Bruno Kreisky, is widely criticized for his decision to honor commitments to the terrorists.

December 17. Members of the NAYLP open fire at the Rome Airport, killing 32 people and wounding another 18. The terrorists commandeer a plane and order it flown to Kuwait, where they surrender to authorities. The original mission was to assassinate Henry Kissinger and break up the Geneva peace conference on the Middle East, but his flight was diverted, so the targets were changed. PLO unhappiness over this incident is apparent when the terrorists are handed over to Libya rather than held for a trial before the PLO. This affair makes evident a schism over strategy that has been developing within the Palestinian movement between moderates and radicals.

December 20. Basque terrorists of the Euskadi Ta Askatasuna (ETA) assassinate the Spanish Premier, Admiral Luis Carrero Blanco, by detonating a bomb under his car. The subsequent police dragnet results in capture or death for most of the ETA leadership, but the assassination ends Franco's attempt to control King Juan Carlos through the right-wing admiral.

1974
May 15. Three members of the Popular Democratic Front for the Liberation of Palestine (PDFLP) seize an Israeli school.

After negotiations break down, Israeli commandos kill the terrorists. During the gun battle, 21 of the 70 children held hostage are killed, along with one of the Israeli commandos. Israel retaliates with a raid against guerrilla camps in southern Lebanon on 16 May.

1974
cont.

May 17. Protestant terrorists from Northern Ireland explode three car bombs in downtown Dublin during the evening rush hour, killing 25 and wounding 180 persons.

August 4. Members of the Italian right-wing terrorist organization, The Black Order, bomb the Rome-to-Munich express train, killing 12 and wounding 48 people. A spokesperson for this act claims it was to protest against the Italian government's ban on fascist groups.

August 19. U.S. Ambassador to Cyprus Rodger P. Davies and a Greek Cypriot embassy secretary killed by Ethniki Organosis Kyprion Agoniston-B (EOKA-B) members during a riot in Nicosia. Three killers identified, because a local film crew covers the assassination. It is three years before the three are tried; two are sentenced to lengthy jail terms.

September 13. Three members of the JRA seize the French embassy in The Hague, taking 11 hostages, including the ambassador, Jacques Senard. Lengthy negotiations result in ransom money and a safe conduct. The terrorists end up in Syria, where they are handed over to the PLO. Some evidence is available that terrorist leader Illich Ramirez Sanchez (Carlos) financed this incident.

October 5. The IRA bombs two Guildford pubs frequented by British soldiers, resulting in 5 deaths and 54 injuries. On November 30, 13 IRA members are arrested for the bombing.

October 31. The left-wing Argentine terrorist group, the Montoneros, bomb the motorboat of Argentina's police chief, Alberto Villar, killing him and his wife. He is assassinated because the Montoneros accuse him of torture and murder of political opponents.

November 13. Yasser Arafat, head of the PLO, speaks before the UN General Assembly. He is accorded the reception of a head of state.

This acceptance by the UN marks a turning point with the PLO leadership as they adopt a more moderate stance on the Israeli-Palestinian issue. In January 1975, the PLO announces that hijackers will be executed if their crimes cause loss of life. Other crimes with no injuries will result in sentences of 15 years hard labor.

1974 November 22. Members of the NAYLP seize a British Airways
cont. VC10 at Dubai with 47 passengers and crew. After killing a West
German passenger, the terrorists are turned over to Tunisia.
The PLO initiates an investigation, and 26 persons in Lebanon
and other Arab countries are arrested. The hijackers are
sentenced by the PLO to long prison terms.

1975 February 27. Members of the West German terrorist group, The
Second of June Movement, kidnap the chairman of the Berlin
Christian Democratic Union (CDU), Peter Lorenz. They hold
him in exchange for five Red Army Faction prisoners. The West
German government complies with the demands, and the
kidnappers and prisoners gain asylum in Aden. Lorenz released
in a West German park.

March 5. Eight members of al-Fatah, the military wing of the
PLO, attack the Hotel Savoy in Tel Aviv, Israel, seizing eight
hostages before the Israeli Defense Force (IDF) overwhelms the
terrorists. Most of the hostages and the terrorists are killed. A
survivor indicates that this action was aimed at sabotaging
upcoming talks between Israel and Egypt.

June 27. The Venezuelan terrorist, Carlos, escapes arrest by the
French police by shooting his way out. He kills two unarmed
policemen and another terrorist. Despite a nationwide dragnet,
Carlos manages to get away.

June 28. Members of the Popular Front for the Liberation of
Palestine—General Command (PFLP-GC), an offshoot of the
PFLP, kidnap a U.S. Army officer, Colonel Ernest R. Morgan, in
Beirut. The terrorists demand food, clothing, and building
supplies to be distributed in Beirut. Morgan released without
the ransom after the PLO threatens retaliation against the
PFLP-GC if Morgan is killed. One explanation for this release is
that it aimed to safeguard Black-American sympathy with the
Palestinian cause.

August 4. Five members of the JRA seize the U.S. consulate in
Kuala Lumpur and hold 52 hostages. While they demand the
release and transportation to Libya of seven prisoners, they win
the release of only five. After lengthy negotiations and some
violence, the terrorists are flown to Libya.

September 15. Four terrorists, probably members of the PFLP,
take over the Egyptian embassy in Madrid.

1975
cont.   They demand that Egypt abandon its negotiations with Israel, and threaten to blow up the embassy and kill the ambassador. Upon their demands, the terrorists and their hostages are flown to Algeria, where they are granted asylum after releasing their hostages.

October 24. The Turkish Ambassador to France, Ismail Erez, and his chauffeur assassinated in Paris by members of the Armenian Revolutionary Army (ASALA). This action was part of an ongoing campaign to attack Turkish targets.

November 27. An IRA gunman kills Ross McWhirter, one of the coeditors of the *Guinness Book of World Records,* in London. McWhirter had offered a $100,000 reward for the arrest of the terrorists responsible for a bombing campaign in London. Four IRA members are sentenced in 1977 to life in prison for this and other murders.

December 2. Seven members of the Free South Moluccan Youth Organization seize a train in Beilen, The Netherlands. The terrorists demand that the Dutch government recognize the Republic of South Molucca and initiate UN mediation on Moluccan independence. Over a 12-day period, three persons are killed before the terrorists release their hostages and surrender to the Dutch police. Each of the seven terrorists receives a 14-year prison sentence.

December 21. The ministers of the Organization of Petroleum Exporting Countries (OPEC) are kidnapped from their Vienna meeting by six members of the PFLP. The terrorist Carlos leads the kidnapping team, which represents a mixture of Palestinians and West Germans. The terrorists demand the broadcast of a manifesto condemning Egyptian-Israeli peace negotiations and an end to all future negotiations with Israel. Permission for this broadcast and a safe-conduct pass is granted by the Austrian government. Both Iran and Saudi Arabia pay large ransoms for their ministers.

The terrorists and their hostages fly to Algeria, where the hostages are released. Algerian authorities allow the terrorists to disappear.

1976   May 11. Members of an obscure terrorist group, Maoist Armed Nuclei for Popular Autonomy, assassinate the Bolivian Ambassador to France, Joaquin Zenteon Anaya.

1976
cont.

The avowed reason for his assassination is that he commanded the troops who captured and executed Ernesto (Ché) Guevara in 1967.

June 16. The U.S. Ambassador to Lebanon, Francis E. Meloy, and two companions kidnaped and murdered in Beirut by unknown Lebanese terrorists.

June 27. Seven members of the PFLP hijack Air France Flight 129 out of Athens. The hijackers, with their 257 hostages, fly the aircraft to Entebbe Airport in Uganda. They demand the release of 53 terrorists from a variety of countries. After nearly a week of negotiations, the terrorists release all but the Jewish hostages. An Israeli commando team storms the airport and frees most of these hostages, though casualties are heavy among the hostages, Israelis, terrorists, and Ugandan soldiers.

July 2. A bomb planted in the dining room of the federal police security building in Buenos Aires by the Montoneros explodes, killing 18 and injuring 66. The Triple A (Argentine Anti-Communist Alliance) retaliate by killing three Irish-born priests, three nuns, and two Argentine seminarians.

July 19. Two leaders of the Argentine left-wing organization, the People's Revolutionary Army (ERP), Roberto Santucho and Enrique Merlo, killed in a gun battle with the police in a suburb of Buenos Aires, Argentina. The loss of two ERP leaders cripples the terrorist campaign.

September 10. TWA Flight 355 hijacked in New York by six Croatian members of the Croatian National Liberation Forces. The terrorists and their hostages fly to Paris where they surrender to French authorities. France extradites the terrorists to the United States. All of the terrorists are sentenced to lengthy prison terms in U.S. jails.

September 21. Orlando Letelier, a former Chilean ambassador to the United States in the Allende government and a critic of the Pinochet regime in Chile, killed along with a minor U.S. government official in a car bombing. Evidence links the Chilean intelligence service and a Cuban anti-Castro terrorist group to the bombing.

October 6. A bomb on Cubana Airlines Flight 455 explodes, killing 73 passengers, most of them Cubans. An anti-Castro terrorist group, Coordination of United Revolutionary Organizations (CORU), claims responsibility.

1976
cont.

CORU's leader Orlando Bosch and his confederates are sentenced to long prison terms in Venezuela for the bombing.

December 1. Members of Abu Nidal's Black June terrorist group shoot and seriously wound the Syrian Foreign Minister, Abdul Halim Khaddam, in Damascus. This attack is in revenge for Syrian intervention in the Lebanese civil war.

December 15. Montoneros terrorists explode a bomb at a Defense Ministry building in Buenos Aires, killing 15 and injuring 30 military officers and civilians.

1977

March 9. Hanafi Muslims seize hostages in a series of coordinated attacks in Washington, DC. After a number of negotiating sessions with this offshoot of the Black Muslims group, the hostages (several of whom are wounded) either escape or are released. All of the active participants receive long prison terms.

April 7. West Germany's chief public prosecutor, Siegfried Buback, assassinated by members of the Red Army Faction. He was the prosecutor in the Baader-Meinhof trials and convictions (see May 24, 1972).

May 23. Members of the South Moluccan independence movement seize a Dutch commuter train between Assen and Groningen, holding 56 passengers hostage. The terrorists demand the release of South Moluccans held in prison for an earlier train hijacking. Dutch commandos assault the train, killing most of the terrorists as well as several of the hostages. The same day these terrorists also seize a school, but the school incident is resolved more peacefully.

September 5. Red Army Faction members kidnap the prominent West German industrialist Hans-Martin Schleyer in Cologne, West Germany. The terrorists demand the release of the leaders of the Red Army Faction held in West German jails. Schleyer is held for 43 days during negotiations, but is killed after the West German government refuses to free the jailed terrorists.

September 28. Five members of the JRA hijack a Japan Air Lines DC8 soon after the plane leaves an Indian airport. The plane and the hostages are diverted to Dacca, Bangladesh. Terrorist demands include release of members of the JRA from prison in Japan and a ransom of $6 million.

1977
cont.

The Japanese government meets the demands, and after a flight to Algeria, the hostages are released and the terrorists surrender to Algerian authorities. Both the Algerian and Japanese governments are criticized for their actions in this incident.

October 13. Lufthansa Flight 181 hijacked near Mallorca by terrorists affiliated with the PFLP-Special Operations, holding 87 passengers and crew. The terrorists demand the freedom of the leaders of the Baader-Meinhof Gang, two Palestinian terrorists, and a ransom of $15 million. After several stops, the aircraft lands at Mogadisu Airport, Somalia. A German commando team, Grenzschutzgruppe Neun (GSG9), storms the aircraft, killing most of the terrorists and freeing the passengers and crew with minimum injuries. The PFLP expels the special operations leader, Dr. Wadi Haddad, in November 1977 over this operation.

October 18. Andreas Baader, Jan-Carl Raspe, and Gudrun Ensslin commit suicide at the maximum security prison at Stammheim, Stuttgart. An investigation by international representatives determines that the deaths were suicides made to look like murders. This finding fails to dispel charges from leftist groups that prison officials murdered the terrorists.

1978

February 18. Unaffiliated terrorists attack the Afro-Asian Peoples' Solidarity Organization in Nicosia, Cyprus, killing Yussef el-Sebai, a newspaper editor and friend of Egyptian President Anwar Sadat and seizing 30 hostages. After their appropriated aircraft is refused landings in several Arab countries, it returns to Cyprus, landing at Larnaca Airport. Egyptian commandos attempt to free the hostages by force, but Cypriot and PLO forces fight off the Egyptians with casualties on both sides. The terrorists then surrender to Cypriot authorities. Egypt suspends diplomatic relations with Cyprus in February 1978 over Cyprus's refusal to turn over the terrorists. The terrorists are sentenced to death, but their sentences are commuted to life imprisonment by the President of Cyprus in February 1978.

March 11. Thirteen terrorists from al-Fatah conduct a sea landing in northern Israel, where they attack several Israeli tourist buses. They kill 46 and wound another 85 people before the IDF ends the incursion. All but two of the terrorists are killed, and these are sentenced to life imprisonment.

1978
cont. The terrorists intended to retard the peace process between
Israel and other Arab states.

March 13. Three South Moluccan terrorists seize a government
building in Assen, The Netherlands, and hold 71 government
employees hostage. They demand the release of South
Moluccan terrorists held in Dutch jails. After negotiations fail,
Dutch marines storm the building, freeing the hostages, with
some casualties, and capturing the terrorists.

March 16. Twelve members of the Italian Red Brigade kidnap
Aldo Moro, the former prime minister and head of the
Christian Democratic Party, after killing his five bodyguards.
The terrorists demand the release of jailed comrades and the
suspension of the Turin trial of 15 Red Brigade leaders. This
kidnapping becomes one of the most famous terrorist incidents
in Europe, and it ends with Moro's death in early May. Twelve
members of the Red Brigade are captured and tried in Italian
courts for their roles in this kidnapping-murder. The resulting
crackdown on the Red Brigade is so intense that it cripples
terrorism in Italy.

August 3. Two PLO officers assassinated in Paris by two
members of the Abu Nidal Group. One of the terrorists is
captured and claims the attack was in protest of Arafat's PLO
policies.

August 22. Twenty-five members of the Sandinista National
Liberation Front (FSLN) seize the national palace in Managua,
Nicaragua. More than 1,500 hostages are taken, including
prominent government officials. Under the leadership of Eden
Pastora (Commander Zero), the FSLN terrorists demand a
general amnesty for all political prisoners and publicity for their
cause. After these demands and a large ransom are met, the
terrorists are allowed safe passage to Mexico and Cuba.

1979 January 22. Ali Hassan Salameh, who helped plan the 1972
Munich Olympic terrorist attack by Black September, is killed by
a car bomb in Beirut. Nine other people also die in the
explosion. Evidence indicates that an Israeli hit team carried out
the bombing-assassination.

February 14. Radical Moslem students attack the U.S. Embassy
in Tehran, Iran, seizing 100 American hostages and beginning a
long hostage ordeal that will last nearly two years.

1979
cont.
Although students lead the original attack, the Iranian government soon becomes an active participant. The conditions for the release of the hostages are the extradition of the exiled Shah of Iran and compensation to Iran, but since the Shah is never turned over to Iran, relations between Iran and the United States deteriorate into mutual hostility. While some hostages are released in November 1979, with maximum media attention, this hostage crisis does not end until January 1981.

February 14. Unidentified terrorists seize the U.S. Ambassador to Afghanistan, Adolph Dubs, and hold him in a Kabul hotel. Dubs dies in the crossfire during a bungled rescue attempt by the Afghanistan police. The three terrorists are also killed in the fighting, leaving the reason for the kidnapping a mystery.

March 22. Either the IRA-Provos or Dutch left-wing sympathizers assassinate the British ambassador to The Hague, Sir Richard Sykes, outside his home in The Hague. Sykes was a security consultant on IRA terrorism and the former British ambassador to the Irish Republic.

March 30. Airey Naeve, Conservative Party specialist on Northern Ireland, killed by a bomb explosion in the underground garage of the House of Commons in London. He was a close friend of Margaret Thatcher. Evidence indicates this bombing was the work of the Irish National Liberation Army (INLA).

July 13. Four members of al-Sa'iga's Red Eagles of the Palestinian Revolution seize the Egyptian Embassy in Ankara, Turkey. Among their demands is Egypt's renunciation of its relations with Israel. The PLO helps in the negotiations with the terrorists. The hostages are released and the terrorists arrested. Some evidence exists that this was a PLO-planned operation.

August 27. Earl Louis Mountbatten of Burma and members of his family killed when an IRA-planted bomb explodes in his fishing boat off the Irish coast. Two IRA members arrested by authorities of the Irish Republic and imprisoned.

1980
January 25. Three members of the African National Congress (ANC) seize the Volkskas bank in Silverton, a white suburb of Pretoria, Republic of South Africa, holding 25 hostages in exchange for the release of black political prisoners, including Nelson Mandela.

1980
cont.

South African police storm the bank, killing the three terrorists. Two hostages are killed and twenty-two others are wounded. Police arrest nine ANC members for their role in planning this incident, and all nine receive lengthy prison terms.

February 27. Members of the left-wing M-19 terrorist group seize the Embassy of the Dominican Republic in Bogotá, Colombia. Among the 45 hostages is the U.S. Ambassador to Colombia, Diego Asencio. The terrorists demand the release of 300 M-19 supporters in prison, $50 million in ransom, and the publication of a manifesto. Negotiations produce the release of nine prisoners and a ransom of $2.5 million; in exchange, most of the hostages are released in April 1980. The terrorists and the remaining hostages are flown to Cuba.

March 24. Catholic Archbishop Oscar A. Romero assassinated during a memorial Mass in San Salvador. Charges are that right-wing hit squads carried out the assassination.

August 2. Italian neofascists explode a bomb in Bologna's main train station, killing 84 and wounding 189. Members of the Armed Revolutionary Nuclei (NAR), Italy's principal right-wing terrorist group, participate in the attack. Sixteen individuals, including several former high-ranking military officers, are arrested and sentenced to long prison terms.

September 12. Members of Omega-7, Cuban-American anti-Castro terrorist group, assassinate a Cuban UN Mission attaché in Queens, New York, by shooting him as he drives his station wagon to work.

September 17. Montoneros assassinate the former Nicaraguan president, Anastasio Somoza Debayle, and two others in Asunción, Paraguay. His car is riddled with machine-gun fire.

September 26. A member of the neo-Nazi paramilitary terrorist group, the Hoffman Military-Sports Group , explodes a grenade at the Munich Oktoberfest beer festival, killing 13 and wounding 215 people. The bomber was also killed in the explosion. Members of the group are arrested for conspiracy by West German police, but most are released for lack of evidence.

December 2. Four U.S. citizens, three Maryknoll order nuns and a Catholic lay social worker, assaulted and murdered outside the International Airport near San Salvador, El Salvador.

1980 Their bodies are found on December 4. After two years of delay,
cont. five National Guardsmen are convicted and sentenced to
lengthy prison terms. Higher-ranking leaders of the right-wing
death squads are implicated but never charged in these murders.

1981 January 3. Three members of the Salvadoran right-wing death
squads assassinate two U.S. citizens, union organizers for the
AFL-CIO, and a Salvadoran peasant union leader in the San
Salvador Sheraton Hotel restaurant. Despite eyewitness
identifications, suspects in the assassination are never brought
to court.

May 13. A Turkish terrorist, Mehmet Ali Agca, with ties to the
Turkish right-wing terrorist group, The Grey Wolves, attempts to
assassinate Pope John Paul II in Saint Peter's Square in the
Vatican. Mehmet Ali Agca had been imprisoned for the murder
of a Turkish journalist, but he had escaped from a Turkish jail.
In a sensational trial, Agca claims that he made the attempt
against the pope for the Bulgarian secret police. After most of
his testimony is discredited, Agca is sentenced to life
imprisonment and the charges against Bulgarian officials are
dropped.

August 29. Two members of the Abu Nidal Group attack the
Synagogue Seitenstettengasse in Vienna with grenades and
machine guns, killing 2 and injuring 20 Jewish worshippers. The
terrorists are sentenced to life imprisonment by Austrian courts.

August 30. A bomb kills the Iranian Prime Minister, Mohammed
Javad Bahonar, and the Iranian president, Mohammed Ali Rajai,
and two others. While no group claims responsibility, the
security chief, Massoud Keshmiri, is blamed.

October 1. Members of the Front for the Liberation of Lebanon
from Foreigners explodes a car bomb in front of the PLO offices in
Beirut, Lebanon. Casualties included 92 persons killed and 250
wounded. Various charges and countercharges are made for the
attack, from blaming the Israelis to the Abu Nidal Group.

October 6. Egyptian President Anwar Sadat assassinated during
a military parade. Nine others are killed during the attack and
another thirty-eight wounded. The assassination is planned and
carried out by members of Islamic fundamentalist groups,
including Atonement and Holy Flight (al-Takfir Wal Higra).

1981
cont.

A fundamentalist Islamic uprising is put down with heavy casualties for both the police and fundamentalists in Asyût the next day. The leading participants in the assassination are executed in April 1982, after a military trial.

October 20. Four members of various U.S. underground terrorist organizations attack a Brinks' armored truck outside a Rockland County, New York, bank. They escape with $1.6 million after a running gun battle with the police. Two policemen and one terrorist are killed in the shootout. Katherine Boudin and Judith Clark, longtime Weather Underground activists, are captured while trying to escape by car. Authorities take the opportunity to raid suspected terrorist hideouts and arrest several more terrorists. Each of those captured receive life terms for this and related crimes.

December 15. A member of the Islamic Jihad drives a car loaded with explosives into the Iraqi embassy in Beirut. The explosion topples a five-story building, killing 61 and injuring more than 100 people. Guards shoot the terrorist just before the bomb explodes, but they are unable to prevent the disaster.

December 17. Members of the Italian Red Brigade kidnap General James Lee Dozier, U.S. officer at the NATO base in Verona. After several terrorist threats to execute Dozier, Italian police rescue him on January 28, 1982. They also capture several of his kidnappers, who decide to cooperate with the police. This cooperation and the Brigade members' numerous lengthy prison sentences will cripple the activities of this terrorist group in the 1980s.

1982

June 3. Four members of the Abu Nidal Group attempt to assassinate the Israeli ambassador to the United Kingdom, Shlomo Argov, in London. Although the terrorists manage to wound the ambassador seriously, they are captured by the police. One of the terrorists is the younger brother of Abu Nidal. Each of the terrorists receives lengthy prison terms.

July 20. Members of the IRA-Provos set off two bombs in London during military changing of the guard ceremonies, killing 9 soldiers and injuring 49 other soldiers and civilians.

July 23. Six foreign tourists kidnapped—two Americans, two Britons, and two Australians—by members of the Zimbabwe African People's Union (ZAPU).

1982
cont.
The terrorists demand the release of two ZAPU leaders undergoing treason trials. Refusing to release the prisoners, the Mugabe government launches a nationwide dragnet. The tourists are killed within three days of their abduction, but their bodies are not found until 1985.

August 7. Members of the Armenian Secret Army for the Liberation of Armenia (ASALA) attack tourists in Esemboga Airport in Ankara, Turkey, killing nine people. The lone surviving terrorist is executed in January 1983.

September 14. President-elect Bashir Gemayel and eight others killed when a large bomb explodes in the Christian Phalangists' office in Beirut. Another 50 people are wounded. The Phalangist Party accuses Habib Tanias Chartouny of the Syrian Socialist Nationalist Party of planting the bomb.

September 17. Twelve members of the left-wing guerrilla organization Chiconeros Popular Liberation Movement seize the Chamber of Commerce building in San Pedrovdel Sula, Honduras. They demand the release of 60 political prisoners in exchange for the 105 hostages they hold. After the terrorists gain safe passage to Cuba, they release the hostages.

1983
April 18. A car bomb explodes at the U.S. Embassy in Beirut, killing 63 and injuring another 88 persons. Among the dead are several prominent U.S. officials. The Islamic Jihad claims responsibility for the attack.

May 20. ANC members explode a car bomb outside the Nedbank Plaza Building in Pretoria, Republic of South Africa. The bomb explodes prematurely and 2 of the 19 people killed in the attack are terrorists. The South African Air Force retaliates by raiding suspected ANC bases near Maput, the capital of Mozambique.

September 23. The Abu Nidal Group claims responsibility for the bombing of a Gulf Air airliner near Abu Dhabi, United Arab Emirates. All 111 passengers are killed, though the apparent target was an aide to the Emir who was not on board as planned.

October 9. North Korean commandos plant a bomb in the Martyr's Mausoleum in Rangoon, Burma, in an attempt to assassinate the South Korean president, Chun Doo Hwan.

1983
cont.
He escapes, but 17 South Korean and Burmese officials are killed and 46 are wounded. Two of the three terrorists are captured, and they confess to acting on orders from North Korean officials. The terrorists are executed.

October 23. Two members of the Islamic Jihad drive trucks loaded with explosives into buildings housing military forces in Beirut. The first truck plows into the U.S. Marine barracks at the Beirut Airport, killing 241 marines. Seconds later in another part of town, an attack on French troops results in 58 more deaths. Both the United States and France recall their forces as a result of these attacks.

December 6. The PLO explodes a bomb under a city bus in Jerusalem, killing 6 passengers and injuring 44.

December 17. Elements among the IRA plant and explode a car bomb outside Harrods Department Store in London. Two policemen are among the 6 killed and 91 wounded in the bombing. A spokesperson for the IRA apologizes for the civilian casualties and claims that this bombing was done without the approval of the leadership of the IRA. A subsequent investigation indicates that the Irish Republican Army Provisional Wing was responsible for the bombing.

1984
January 18. Malcolm Kerr, president of the American University of Beirut in Lebanon, assassinated by two members of the Islamic Jihad. This group considers him a bad influence on Lebanese students.

March 16. Thomas Buckley, the political officer at the U.S. Embassy in Beirut and CIA station chief, kidnapped by members of the Islamic Jihad. Evidence indicates that he died on June 3, 1985 as a result of torture. His body is returned to authorities in January 1992.

June 18. Right-wing terrorists of the Silent Brotherhood assassinate radio talk show host Alan Berg in Denver, Colorado. The leader of the Silent Brotherhood, Robert Jay Mathews, regards Berg as part of a Zionist conspiracy.

October 12. The IRA-Provos explode a bomb at a London hotel in an attempt to wipe out the British government. Margaret Thatcher escapes unhurt, but 4 government officials and 40 others are injured.

1984
cont.

October 31. Prime Minister Indira Gandhi assassinated by two members of her Sikh bodyguards, Beant Singh and Satwant Singh. The Sikhs are acting in revenge for the military crackdown of the Sikhs and the storming of the Golden Temple of Amritsar. In the aftermath of the assassination, between 2,500 and 5,000 Sikhs are massacred in several days of rioting throughout India. Beant Singh is murdered in police custody. Satwant Singh is hanged in January 1989 for the assassination.

December 3. A Kuwaiti aircraft hijacked by Lebanese terrorists and flown to Tehran, Iran. The terrorists hold 166 hostages. After killing two USAID employees, the terrorists begin releasing hostages in stages until the Iranian authorities attack the plane and free the last nine hostages. Some conjecture remains that the terrorists had the support of the Iranian government in this hijacking.

December 3. Peter Kilburn, a librarian at the American University of Beirut, kidnapped by terrorists in Beirut. His body is found in October 1986 along with those of two British teachers who had also been kidnapped.

December 8. Robert Jay Mathews, leader of the American rightist group, the Silent Brotherhood, killed in a police shootout on Whidbey Island, Washington. His confederates are rounded up and most receive lengthy federal prison sentences.

1985

March 1. IRA terrorists launch mortar rounds into a police barracks in Newry, Northern Ireland, killing 9 members of the Royal Ulster Constabulary and wounding 37 others.

March 8. Terrorists trained by the CIA explode a car bomb in Beirut, killing 92 people. The target is Sheikh Muhammed Hassan Fadlallah, a Shi'ite leader, but he escapes injury in the blast.

March 16. Associated Press reporter Terry Anderson kidnapped in Beirut and is held by the Islamic Jihad until December 4, 1991. He is the last of the American hostages released because his captors value him as a negotiating pawn.

April 21. Members of al-Fatah attempt a seaborne assault on Israel. Their ship, the *Alavarius* is intercepted and sunk by the Israeli Navy; 20 terrorists drown and 8 more are captured.

1985
cont.

June 9. Thomas Sutherland, dean of agriculture at the American University of Beirut, kidnapped by members of the Islamic Jihad. He is released on November 18, 1991, along with Terry Waite (an Anglican emissary who was kidnapped later—see January 20, 1987).

June 14. TWA Flight 847 from Athens to Rome hijacked by Lebanese terrorists. Most of the hostages are Americans. After the murder of a U.S. Navy diver, Robert Stethem, negotiations at the Beirut Airport conclude with Israel releasing Shi'ite prisoners in exchange for the hostages. During the last stages, the hostages are held by the Amal and the Hezbollah groups. One of the hijackers, Mohammed Ali Hamadei, is arrested in 1987 in West Germany and tried for his part in this hijacking.

June 19. Members of the Central American Revolutionary Workers Party shoot and kill 13 people at an outdoor cafe in San Salvador. Among those killed are four marines and two U.S. businessmen.

June 21. An Air India Boeing 747 crashes near the Irish coast from the explosion of a plastic bomb planted by Sikh terrorists. All 329 passengers are killed. Both Sikh terrorists and the Kashmir Liberation Army claim responsibility for the bomb.

October 7. Four terrorists, members of the Tunis-based faction of the PLF under Abdul Abbas, seize the Italian cruise ship *Achille Lauro* off Port Said, Egypt. Among the 400 people held hostage are 12 Americans, and one of them, Leon Klinghoffer, is killed. After the ship returns to Egypt, the hijackers surrender to PLO and Egyptian officials. When the Egyptian government releases the terrorists, the U.S. Navy intercepts the hijackers' plane and forces it down in Italy, where the hijackers are arrested. This seizure of the terrorists causes an international crisis.

November 6. Members of the Colombian M-19 terrorist group seize the Palace of Justice in Bogotá, Colombia. The terrorists hold 100 hostages, including most of Colombia's legal establishment. Colombian military forces storm the palace with heavy casualties. Ninety-three judges, civilians, and terrorists are killed in the assault.

November 23. Unknown terrorists, probably with links to Colonel Qaddafi, hijack an Egypt Air Boeing 737 on a flight from Athens to Cairo.

1985
cont.   The plane lands at Luqa, Malta, where the Egyptian antiterrorist "Thunderbolt" force assaults the plane to free the hostages. Nine people, including the terrorists, die when the plane catches fire.

1986   February 28. An unknown terrorist assassinates the Prime Minister of Sweden, Olaf Palme, in midtown Stockholm. Several terrorist groups claim credit, but the case is still open. Some suspicion for this assassination has centered on Kurdish groups .

April 14. U.S. Air Force aircraft bomb Tripoli, Libya, in retaliation for Qaddafi's sponsorship of terrorist attacks against U.S. forces in West Germany. While military targets are hit, 60 civilians are also killed. Most countries, including the United States' NATO allies, condemn the attack, but Qaddafi has maintained a lower profile in his sponsorship of terrorism since the attack.

May 3. Members of the Liberation Tigers of Tamil Eelam explode a bomb in an Air Lanka Tristar airplane in Colombo, Sri Lanka, killing 17 people. Three of the victims are British tourists, and the Thatcher government retaliates by aiding the Sri Lanka government, which the Tamils oppose.

June 26. Members of Peru's left-wing Shining Path (Sendero Luminoso) plant a bomb aboard a tourist train bound for the Inca ruins of Machu Picchu. Seven people are killed and many others injured.

July 9. Members of the Red Army Faction assassinate Dr. Karl-Heinz Beckurts, an executive of Siemens Company, with a remote-controlled bomb. He is killed because of his involvement with the nuclear industry and research into the Strategic Defense Initiative.

September 6. Two members of the Abu Nidal Group attack the Neve Shalom Synagogue in Istanbul, killing 22 persons and wounding 7 others before blowing themselves up.

September 12. Four terrorists kidnap Joseph Cicippio, the comptroller of the American University of Beirut, outside his home in Beirut. He is held hostage by the Shi'ite Revolutionary Justice Organization. After several threats to execute him, Cicippio is released on December 2, 1991.

1986
cont.

He is freed one day after Israel released 25 Arab prisoners from Khiam prison in southern Lebanon.

November 17. Members of Action Directe assassinate Georges Besse, the president of Renault, in Paris. He is attacked because of his earlier role in developing the French nuclear industry.

December 25. Terrorists attempt a hijacking of an Iraqi airliner in Saudi Arabia, but the plane crashes. Only 45 of the 107 people aboard survive the crash. Iranian-backed terrorists are probably responsible.

1987

January 20. Anglican layman Terry Waite, the personal emissary of the Archbishop of Canterbury, kidnapped by the Islamic Jihad in the midst of negotiations for the release of hostages Terry Anderson and Thomas Sutherland. Newspaper reports claiming that the CIA is gaining information about the terrorists from Waite's contacts with the kidnappers seems to have triggered his kidnapping. He is released on November 18, 1991 as part of the relaxation of tensions before the Arab-Israeli peace talks in Madrid, Spain.

January 24. Alann Steen, a communications professor at Beirut University, kidnapped by terrorists in Beirut. He is freed by his captors, the Islamic Jihad, on 3 December 1991.

February 21. French police arrest the four top leaders of Action Directe in a farmhouse near Orleans.

April 19. A shootout between members of the al-Fatah and the Israeli Defense Force on the Lebanese-Israeli border results in the deaths of two Israeli soldiers and three Palestinian guerrillas.

April 21. Tamil guerrillas explode a bomb in a bus station in Colombo, Sri Lanka, during rush hour. The bomb kills 105 people and injures 200 others.

June 2. Lebanese Prime Minister Rashid Karami assassinated when a bomb explodes in his military helicopter. A terrorist group, the Lebanese Secret Army, claims responsibility.

June 20. Members of the ETA explode a bomb in a department store parking garage in Barcelona, Spain. The explosion kills 17 people and wounds another 39.

1987
cont.
July 6. Sikh terrorists ambush a bus near Chandigarh, India, and kill 36 Hindu passengers. More than 500 people have been killed in violence between Hindu and Sikh extremists in the first six months of 1987.

November 8. Members of the IRA-Provos detonate a bomb at a British war memorial ceremony in Enniskillen, Northern Ireland, killing 11 people. More than 60 others are injured.

November 29. Korean Air Lines Flight 858 crashes into the Andaman Sea of Burma as the result of a bomb explosion. Two North Korean intelligence agents are arrested for the bombing, and one confesses and explains it is to destabilize the South Korean government and disrupt the 1988 Olympic Games in Seoul.

1988
February 17. Marine Lieutenant Colonel William Higgins, commander of the UN Truce Supervisory Organization in Lebanon, is kidnapped by terrorists. His kidnappers claim he is executed in late July 1989 in retaliation for Israel's abduction of Hezbollah cleric Sheikh Abdul Karim Obeid, but he is believed to have died under torture several months earlier. His body is released in January 1992.

April 5. A Kuwaiti airliner with more than 110 people aboard hijacked on a flight from Bangkok to Kuwait by members of the pro-Iranian fundamentalist group, the Hezbollah. The aircraft first lands in Iran and then flies to Cyprus. Hijacker demands include safe passage and the release of 17 terrorists held in Kuwaiti jails for a 1983 bombing attack. Several times, the hijackers release passengers to indicate good faith, but they also execute two passengers when the imprisoned terrorists are not released by their deadlines. On the eighth day of the hijacking the aircraft is flown to Algeria. The Algerian government allows safe passage out of Algeria for the terrorists in return for the release of the remaining hostages.

April 14. Members of the JRA bomb a CSO club in Naples, Italy. The explosion kills five people, including an American soldier. This incident marks the reappearance of the JRA as a significant terrorist force after a long period of dormancy.

May 1. A bus crowded with shoppers is blown up by Tamil terrorists near a village in Sri Lanka, killing 26 people.

1988
cont.
This incident is typical of terrorist activity in Sri Lanka in 1988, until the Indian Army intervenes.

August 17. A Pakistani Air Force plane explodes in midair, killing President Mohammad Zia ul-Haq of Pakistan and the U.S. Ambassador to Pakistan, Arnold L. Raphel. A total of 30 people are killed in the explosion and crash. Nine Pakistani Air Force officers are arrested on suspicion of planting a bomb, but no evidence is ever found. Various investigations are inconclusive about the cause of the explosion, but sabotage is the most likely scenario. The loss of President Zia changes the direction of politics in Pakistan.

October 19. Seven Israeli soldiers are killed and eight wounded in a car-bomb attack in southern Lebanon. A pro-Iranian group in Beirut, Islamic Resistance, claims responsibility.

December 21. A Pan Am Boeing 747 en route to New York from Frankfurt is rocked by a bomb and crashes in Lockerbie, Scotland. All 258 people on board are killed, as well as 11 people in Lockerbie. An investigation concludes that the bomb was placed in a radio-cassette player and packed in with the luggage in Frankfurt. Further study by terrorist experts concludes that the PFLP-General Command is responsible for the bombing. Evidence discovered in 1992 leads both British and American governments to attempt trying two Libyan intelligence agents, Abdel Baset Ali al-Mehrahi and Lamen Khalifa Fhima.

1989
March 4. Shining Path guerrillas kill 39 people in a remote mountain village in Peru. The killings are in revenge for the creation of a peasant patrol to fight the guerrillas.

April 13. Tamil terrorists explode a car bomb in a crowded marketplace in Trincomalee, Sri Lanka, killing 38 shoppers and wounding 56 others. In a retaliatory attack, five Tamils are killed later in the day by Sinhalese.

May 16. Sheikh Hassan Khaled, religious leader of Sunni Muslims in Lebanon, is assassinated by a car bomb in west Beirut. Casualties include 21 other people killed and more than 100 injured. He was considered a political moderate in the struggle for political control of Lebanon.

1989
cont.

September 22. IRA terrorists explode a bomb at the barracks of the British marines' music school in Walmer, England, killing 10 people.

November 22. Lebanese President René Moawad is assassinated by a car bomb in an explosion that kills at least 23 other people. He is a Maronite Christian and a political moderate who was president for only 17 days. No organization claims responsibility for his assassination so the blame falls on the followers of the Maronite Christian leader General Michel Aoun.

November 30. Members of the Red Army Faction assassinate the head of West Germany's largest commercial bank, Alfred Herrhausen, in a car bomb explosion. He is considered the most powerful person in West Germany's economy.

1990

February 4. Terrorists assault a tour bus carrying a group of Israeli academics and their wives east of Cairo, Egypt. The terrorists kill 9 Israelis and wound 17 others. Palestinian guerrillas are suspected in the attack, and relations between Egypt and the PLO are strained over this incident.

July 30. Ian Gow, Conservative member of the British Parliament, is killed when a car bomb explodes outside his home in the London suburb of Hankham. He was an outspoken critic of the IRA and a close friend of Prime Minister Thatcher. The IRA claims responsibility for the bombing.

August 4. Tamil terrorists assault two Muslim mosques in eastern Sri Lanka, killing more than 110 worshippers. This incident is another in a series of terrorist acts by the Tamils that claimed nearly 1,000 lives during 1990.

November 5. Rabbi Meir Kahane, founder of the Jewish Defense League, is gunned down by a terrorist during a Zionist Conference at a New York City hotel. The gunman is identified later as El Sayyid a Nosair, an Egyptian-born air conditioner repairman. Riots break out in Israel over his death. Despite eyewitness accounts, El Sayyid is not convicted of the assassination in a sensational court trial in 1991.

1991

January 14. Two high-ranking PLO aides, Saleh Khalef, second-in-command in the PLO, and Hayel Abdel-Hamid, the security chief for the PLO, are assassinated by Hamza Abu Zaid, a bodyguard.

1991
cont.

Khalef was the former head of Black September and the heir apparent to Arafat in the PLO. The Abu Nidal Group is implicated in both of these deaths.

March 2. A car bomb explodes in Colombo, Sri Lanka, killing 19 people and wounding about 73 others. Deputy Defense Minister Ranjan Wijeratne, who led the fight against the Tamil rebels, is among the victims. Tamil terrorists are suspected, but Wijeratne also had enemies among the Sinhalese community.

March 4. Members of the Ulster Volunteer Force, a Protestant paramilitary corps, assumes responsibility for the murder of four Roman Catholics and the wounding of another in an attack on a village pub in Northern Ireland.

April 2. Detlev Rohwedder, head of the German agency (Treuhand) privatizing the East German economy, is killed in his home in Dusseldorf. Authorities suspect members of the Red Army Faction for the assassination. This act starts a campaign by terrorists to stop privatizing of East German businesses.

April 19. Palestinian terrorists explode a parcel bomb at the British consulate in Athens, Greece, killing seven and wounding eight others. Seven Palestinians are arrested and held for trial by Greek authorities and 26 Palestinian diplomats and students are expelled from the country.

May 21. Former Indian Prime Minister Rajiv Gandhi assassinated in the southern Indian town of Sriperambudur near Madras, India. At least 17 other people are killed as a woman assassin blew up herself and others with nitro-based explosives. Gandhi was campaigning in a national election to return to power with the Congress Party. Although the exact motivation is uncertain, the woman was a member of the Liberation Tigers of Tamil Eelam (LTTE). Efforts to identify other members of the plot have been hindered by suicides of suspects.

June 1. Members of the IRA explode a truck full of explosives at a small Ulster Defense Regiment base in Glenanne, Northern Ireland. Three soldiers are killed and another 10 wounded.

August 8. British journalist and hostage, John McCarthy, is released by his terrorist captives in Beirut, Lebanon. He had been held hostage for five years.

1991
cont.

This action is widely interpreted as the first step in placing pressure on Israel to free its 300–400 Arab prisoners.

September 11. Israel releases 51 Lebanese captives and nine bodies as a humanitarian gesture. UN chief Javier Perez de Cuellar is credited with engineering this release.

September 12. Unidentified terrorists conduct hit-and-run attacks on commuters for three days in townships near Johannesburg, South Africa. Nearly 100 people are killed. Rivalry between the ANC and the Inkatha Freedom Party is blamed for the terrorism.

September 24. British hostage, Jack Mann, is released by the Revolutionary Justice Organization after nearly two and a half years of captivity.

October 22. American hostage, Jesse Turner, is released from captivity by the Islamic Jihad in Beirut, Lebanon. He had been held for four years and ten months.

November 18. American hostage, Thomas Sutherland, and the Anglican Church envoy, Terry Waite, are released in Beirut, Lebanon, by the Islamic Jihad. Their release is interpreted by British and U.S. authorities to indicate that Iran wants its Shi'ite allies in Lebanon to liberate their hostages in an effort to improve relations with the West.

December 3. Joseph Cicippio and Alann Steen end their years of captivity in Beirut, Lebanon.

December 4. The last remaining U.S. hostage, Terry Anderson, is released in Beirut, Lebanon. He spent six years and nine months as a hostage. His release ends the political drama between the United States and the Shi'ite fundamentalists over American hostages.

December 22. Members of the Ulster Freedom Fighters, a Protestant terrorist organization, plant firebombs in London's underground rail system. Firebombs are removed with little damage and few casualties. This act is in retaliation for shootings by the IRA in Protestant Belfast neighborhoods.

1992 February 14. Members of the Maoist Shining Path organization blow up a police van in Lima, Peru, killing four policemen and wounding five others. This action is one of a series of terrorist acts by the Shining Path as it intensifies its terrorist campaign, moving into urban areas.

March 17. The killing of Hezbollah leader Sheik Abbas Mussawi by an Israeli strike team in southern Lebanon reopens hostilities on the Israeli-Lebanese border. Mussawi's wife, young son, and five bodyguards are also killed. Other members of Hezbollah's leadership vow revenge.

March 18. Terrorists of the Islamic Jihad plant a bomb at the Israeli embassy in Buenos Aires, Argentina. The explosion kills 25 and injures 252. Despite the short time between this bombing and Mussawi's death, this act may have been in retaliation for Mussawi's killing.

April 10. An IRA car bomb explodes in London's financial district. Two people are killed and 80 injured.

June 29. Unknown terrorists assassinate the Algerian president of the High State Committee, Mohamed Boudiaf. Authorities suspect members of the Islamic Salvation Front, a Muslim fundamentalist movement, of plotting the assassination. Boudiaf had been a leader in the Algerian independence movement and a national hero.

June 30. Italian prison authorities release Alberto Franceschini, one of the founders and leaders of the Red Brigade, after he serves 18 years of a 30-year sentence for terrorism. Part of the terms for his release was a pledge by Franceschini to renounce terrorism.

3

Biographical Profiles of Leading Terrorists, 1945–1992

TERRORISTS CRAVE PUBLICITY for their causes because they seek an audience to justify both their causes and their actions. Terrorists also believe that the righteousness of their causes justifies any means they use to gain them. Still, for obvious reasons, they are less enthusiastic about personal publicity. Too much publicity about an individual terrorist, or details about a group's activities, can give security forces or the police clues to catching the individual or infiltrating the group. The few terrorists who do not live by this tenet usually do not last long. Consequently, scholars studying terrorists must sift through misinformation, or incomplete information. Sometimes background information about individual terrorists comes out of police interrogations or court trials, but this type of information appears only infrequently. Occasionally, a terrorist will grant an interview, and rarely, he or she will publish memoirs. While these memoirs are usually self-justifications, they do give insight into the motivations of a particular terrorist. The life expectancy of a terrorist is short, so it is difficult to discover personal information before the person's demise. Though some details may be sketchy or lacking, the following list includes biographical sketches of some of the most notorious and influential terrorists of the last half century. While this list of terrorists is highly selective, it gives a profile of major terrorists and their roles in the terrorist movement. Women are heavily represented here because women have played a significant role in most left-wing terrorist organizations. Several organizations have had women leaders or women in positions to determine policy.

Naji Alesh (Palestine)

Alesh is one of the principal theorists of the Palestinian movement. As early as the 1950s, he advocated the creation of a Palestinian state by Palestinians. In his book, *The Road to Palestine*, he formed the ideological basis for Palestinian guerrilla fighters. Along with his position on the Palestinian National Council of the Palestine Liberation Organization (PLO), he was the secretary general of the General Union of Palestinian Writers. His views often conflicted with those of Yasser Arafat, but Arafat was powerless to do anything about it until Alesh left the PLO to join forces with Abu Nidal in 1978. Alesh disagreed with Abu Nidal in 1979, and he left Iraq to join Qaddafi in Libya. He no longer plays a prominent role in determining policy, but his place as a theorist for Palestinian national liberation remains secure.

Yasser Arafat (Palestine)

Arafat has led the PLO since the late 1960s. Conflicting reports on Arafat's birthplace and family have circulated. His real name is Abdel-Rahman Abdel-Raout Arafat al-Qudwa Al-Husseini. The most reliable sources indicate that he was born on August 24, 1929 of wealthy Sunni Muslim Palestinian parents in Cairo, Egypt. His family was related to the powerful Husseini family. During his youth, he alternated between living in Cairo and Jerusalem, but he was educated in Egyptian schools. During the 1948 war, the Arafat family was in Jerusalem after which they moved to Gaza. He returned to Egypt in the early 1950s to study engineering at King Faud University. Some evidence indicates that he served as a lieutenant in the Egyptian army during the 1956 Suez War. Arafat also became active in the Muslim Brotherhood, an Egyptian ultraconservative religious and political organization, for which he was jailed during President Nasser's crackdown on the group. In 1957, Arafat and seven confederates founded the terrorist organization al-Fatah. After nearly a decade of leading the group, he assumed the leadership post of the PLO. Despite an occasional breakaway group, the PLO has long been acknowledged as the official voice of the Palestinian people. Arafat has always been careful to surround himself in the PLO with friends from al-Fatah so that leadership challenges have been minimal. The 1973 war caused Arafat to change the activities of the PLO from international terrorism to more peaceful political efforts to isolate Israel and bring about a Palestinian state through negotiation. His address at the UN General Assembly in November 1974 was part of this new strategy. Arafat's conciliatory stance, however, produced a variety of rejectionist groups, some of which have attempted to assassinate him. He has remained the leader of the PLO despite the ouster of the PLO leadership from Lebanon in the mid-1980s. His pro-Iraqi position during the Persian Gulf War in 1991 weakened his influence with the conservative Arab states and lost the group its financial support from Kuwait. Still, Arafat has proved himself a survivor, and his identification with the PLO continues to be strong. His role after the Arab-Israeli peace conference in early 1992 remains uncertain.

Arafat suffered a head injury in an aircraft crash in Libya in April 1992. A subsequent operation for the injury caused considerable uncertainty about his role in the PLO. The reaction by Palestinians to his apparent recovery from the operation and the lack of an annointed successor seem to cement Arafat's indispensability as a PLO leader.

Andreas Baader (West Germany)

Baader was one of the principal leaders of the West German terrorist organization, the Red Army Faction (RAF). Born in Munich on May 6, 1943, his father was a historian who was killed fighting in the last days of World War II. Unlike most left-wing terrorists, he never finished high school, and his early career in Berlin seems to have been most distinguished by his love affairs. His leadership abilities became apparent when he joined the fringe of the West German radical student movement. Baader became one of the leaders of the German Socialist Student Alliance (SDS). When the SDS split into various factions, he was introduced to terrorism through his girlfriend, Gudrun Ensslin (see entry). Their first operation was the 1968 bombing of a department in Frankfurt. Several times Baader was arrested by the West German police, but he always escaped. While he received training in terrorist tactics in Lebanon from the Palestine Front for the Liberation of Palestine (PFLP), Baader was not considered one of their better students. He was finally captured by the West German police in 1972. After an attempt to win his release failed in 1977, he committed suicide on October 18, 1977, in his maximum security prison cell at Stammheim Prison. Enough uncertainty remains over his suicide that he has become a martyr to many European terrorists.

Menachem Begin (Israel)

Begin's political career began as the head of the Jewish terrorist organization, Irgun Zvai Leumi (National Military Organization), and ended as the prime minister of Israel. He was born on 16 August 1913 in Brest-Litovsk, Poland, into a family of timber merchants. In the Polish schools, he experienced anti-Semitism. He and his wife, Aliza, fled from Poland to the Soviet Union in 1939. After serving some time in a Soviet prison camp as a suspected dissident, Begin joined the Free Polish Army of Wladyslaw Anders. Because of difficulty with Stalin, Anders's army moved to Palestine in 1942, and Begin went with it. Most of Begin's family was murdered by the Nazis, and he blamed the British almost as much as he did the Nazis. Begin soon became active in the Irgun and assumed a leadership role, waging a selective campaign of terror against British police and government offices during the mid-1940s. His most famous act was the bombing of the King David Hotel in Jerusalem in July 1946. After the creation of the state of Israel, Begin began a political career forming the Herut (Freedom) Movement, a political party on the extreme right of Israeli politics. He was elected to the Israeli Parliament, the Knesset, in 1948. In 1973, he was instrumental in forming the nationalistic and influential Likud (Unity) Party. His successes in the Knesset led to his election as prime minister in 1977, a position he held until 1983 (he was also the minister of defense during 1980–1981). In 1978, Begin was the recipient of the Nobel Peace Prize. Begin published his memoirs, *The Revolt: Personal Memoirs of the Commander of Irgun Zvai Leumi* (1949), to outline his life as a terrorist. Begin served as the elder statesman of the Likud Party until his death in Jerusalem on March 9, 1992.

Mohammed Boudia (Algeria)

Boudia was one of the leaders of the Palestinian terrorist organization Black September, whose job was to coordinate the activities of several left-wing terrorist groups in Europe. He was born in Algeria and had been a member of the National Front for the Liberation of Algeria (FLN), spending three years in a French prison. After his release from jail, Boudia became active in Algerian politics as a member of a Marxist group opposed to Boumedienne's regime in Algeria. The Palestinian cause also attracted him, and he trained at Patrice Lumumba University in Moscow. Soon after this training Boudia became one of the most prominent operatives for George Habash's PFLP (see entry) in Europe. He has also been accused of being a KGB operative working under the control of Yuri Kotov, a veteran KGB agent, but this has never been proven. His position as the manager of the Theatre de l'Ouest in Paris gave him access to French left-wing intellectuals. In 1972, Boudia switched allegiance and joined Black September. His ability to recruit French women for various Black September operations helped him in his mission to coordinate terrorist operations. His friendship with fellow terrorist, Carlos (see entry below), helped him conduct a European terrorist network. He was killed on June 28, 1973 in Paris by a car bomb planted by the Israeli Wrath of God counterterrorist group in retaliation for his leading role in the 1972 Munich Olympic terrorist operation.

Pierre Carette (Belgium)

Carette is the founder and leader of the Belgian terrorist group, the Communist Combatant Cells (CCC). He was born into a working-class family in Charleroi, Belgium, in 1952. His profession as a printer brought him early into close contact with left-wing figures in Brussels, Mons, and Charleroi. It was the activities of the RAF in West Germany in the early 1970s that inspired him to join several related organizations. His dissatisfaction with the moderate policies of the Belgian left caused him to leave these organizations in the late 1970s. In 1979, Carette started a cooperative printing establishment to promote his political views. Among the publications was the journal *Subversion*. He also began to work toward the formation of a Belgian urban guerrilla group, but his estrangement from other left-wing groups made it difficult for him to attract followers. Only by joining a fringe group, the Internationalist Communist Front, did he become involved in terrorist politics. Completing his education on terrorism, Carette met the French militant theorist Frederic Oriach in 1982. Oriach also introduced him to the founders of the French terrorist group, Action Directe, Jean-Marc Rouillan (see entry) and Nathalie Menignon. It was under the sponsorship of Oriach, Rouillan, and Menignon that Carette founded the CCC in 1982, using robberies to finance additional operations. Belgium was in the midst of a political controversy over the stationing of cruise missiles, so Carette made NATO installations CCC's primary targets. Between October 1984 and December 1985, the group committed 20 terrorist acts against property; about half involved NATO facilities. Sometime during

1983–1984, Carette broke with his friends in the Action Directe over tactics. In the middle of his terrorist campaign in December 1985, Carette was arrested with three other members of his group by the Belgian police. Carette is now serving a lengthy prison term in a Belgian prison with little hope of an early parole.

Renato Curcio (Italy)

Curcio is one of the most important leaders of the Italian terrorist group, the Red Brigade. Educated in good Italian schools, he then studied sociology at the University of Trent. His initial political interest was with the Italian right-wing terrorist organization, the New Order. He soon changed his orientation toward left-wing groups, and, by the early 1970s, he was involved in terrorist activities. Renato was captured by the police in 1974, but his wife (Margherita Cagol) organized his escape later that year. He was finally arrested in 1976, but he was not tried until 1978. His followers pursued a policy of intimidation of the Italian judicial system, attacking and killing several important officials. He is presently serving a life sentence in an Italian jail for his terrorist activities.

Bernardine Dohrn (United States)

Dohrn was one of the leaders of the American terrorist group, the Weather Underground. She was born in 1942 near Chicago, Illinois, and grew up in a suburb of Milwaukee. After a normal high school career, Dohrn attended first the University of Miami (Ohio) and then the University of Chicago. Upon graduating from law school in 1967, she moved to New York to join the legal staff of the National Lawyers Guild. It was in New York City that she became acquainted with members of the Students for a Democratic Society (SDS) and soon became one of its leaders. She led the left wing of the SDS into a new group called the Weathermen (original name of the Weather Underground). Her role as a militant leader in the Weathermen became apparent during the four "Days of Rage" in Chicago in October 1969. In the aftermath of the crackdown, Dohrn went underground with many of her colleagues. In the next few years, the Weather Underground launched a series of bombing attacks. Dohrn earned a place on the FBI's "Ten Most Wanted" list, but she evaded capture for nearly 20 years, finally surrendering on her own.

Gudrun Ensslin (West Germany)

Ensslin gained fame as the operational commander of the Red Army Faction. She was born at Berthomomae, Swabia, on August 15, 1940, the daughter of a Lutheran minister. After a brilliant academic record, she attended the universities of Tübingen and Berlin where she passed her teacher's examinations. Ensslin gave birth to a child by fellow German student, Bernhard Vester, who was later to commit suicide. While at college, she became a member of the German SDS. She became acquainted with another radical, Andreas Baader (see entry), and they became lovers. After a failed assassination attempt against the West German student leader, Rudi Dutschke, Ensslin and Baader began to agitate for a counterstrike against the state. By this time, Ensslin had befriended Ulrike Meinhof (see entry). Together with her friends, Ensslin participated in an active terrorist campaign in West Germany. She was arrested by German police and sentenced to a long prison term. She committed suicide at the same time as Baader in 1977. Ensslin never had the same reputation as a terrorist as her colleagues in the Red Army Faction, but in many ways she was the most dedicated terrorist of the group.

Frantz Fanon (Martinique)

Fanon remains one of the foremost theorists advocating wars of national liberation. Fanon was born in Martinique and was well educated. He fought for the Free French in France and Africa during World War II. After receiving a French degree in psychiatry, he moved to Algeria to practice his profession. Several years later he joined the Front de Liberation Nationale (FLN) to win Algerian independence from French control. He became the leading theorist for the FLN, and the French attempted to assassinate him several times. A severe critic of colonialism and racial oppression, he wrote a book, *The Wretched of the Earth,* that became influential for advocating violence against oppression. Although he died of leukemia in Washington, D.C. in December 1961, several years before Algeria gained its independence, he is still quoted and studied by supporters of wars of national liberation and by terrorists. His writings especially influenced the U.S. Black Panther Party.

Giangiacomo Feltrinelli (Italy)

Feltrinelli served as the financial sponsor and leading instigator of Italian left-wing terrorism in the 1960s and early 1970s. He was born in 1926 into the fabulously wealthy and influential Feltrinelli family. His education was provided by family tutors until his stepfather, the famous novelist Luigi Barzini, sent him to a state school in Milan. In his early youth, Feltrinelli was an ardent fascist, but the fall of Mussolini ended this devotion, and he served with distinction in the Italian Liberation Army in 1945. After the war, he joined the Italian Communist Party. He also launched a successful career as a publisher, mostly of left-wing writers. When he published an Italian version of Boris Pasternak's *Dr. Zhivago,* it caused strife with the Italian Communist Party leadership. As a result, Feltrinelli resigned from the party in 1957. Despite this open break, Feltrinelli maintained his contacts in left-wing and Communist circles. His interest in Latin American guerrillas led him to make several trips to Cuba and he befriended Fidel Castro. He also established personal contact with terrorist leaders in the Middle East and in West Germany by supplying them with financing and weapons. His frequent trips to Czechoslovakia suggest that his relationship with the Communist Party continued. In December 1969, Feltrinelli went underground to form the Italian terrorist group, the Proletarian Action Group. He was instrumental in recruiting disaffected students and middle-class professionals to the terrorist ranks and in locating financial resources to carry out terrorist operations. He was considered one of Europe's leading advocates of left-wing terrorism until his accidental death on March 15, 1972 during a terrorist bombing attempt in northern Italy. His loss was a serious blow to both Italian and European terrorism, and many of his followers transferred into the Red Brigade afterward.

George Grivas (Cyprus)

Grivas was military commander of the Greek Cypriot terrorist group, Ethniki Organosis Kyprion Agoniston (EOKA). He was born on Cyprus, but most of his military career was spent in the Greek Army. He served as an officer during the Greek-Turkish War in the early 1920s and during World War II. Grivas had retired as a colonel in the Greek Army when he returned to Cyprus in 1954. His political views consisted of a staunch anti-Communism, faith in the Orthodox Church, and a belief in expansionary Hellenism. These views led him to form the terrorist organization EOKA to fight for Enosis (union with Greece) for Cyprus. He allied with the Cypriot political leader Archbishop Makarios, and together they conducted a violent terrorist campaign against British forces eventually making it too risky for them to remain in Cyprus. Grivas organized his forces into three fighting groups: mountain guerrillas, village groups, and town groups. More than a thousand terrorists targeted British personnel for assassination, bombings, and harassment during nearly five years, with hundreds of casualties. Grivas managed to escape arrest even after the British launched massive manhunts to find him. A political settlement was finally concluded between the British and Archbishop Makarios, but, since it did not contain the union of Cyprus with Greece, Grivas remained lukewarm over the settlement. He commanded the Cypriot National Guard from 1964 to 1967, but he became so politically dangerous that he was finally exiled to Greece. In 1971, Grivas returned to Cyprus and he reconstituted his terrorist campaign, but this time Makarios opposed him. His new terrorist organization, EOKA -B, was less successful than his earlier group, but it did constitute a constant danger to the Makarios government. Grivas died on January, 27 1974, in Limassol, Cyprus, of a heart attack. His absence and a Turkish invasion finally crushed his movement.

Ernesto (Ché) Guevara de la Serna (Argentina)

Ché Guevara has been described as "the wandering minstrel of revolution," but he gained most of his fame in fighting with Fidel Castro in the Cuban Revolution of 1959 and in his death leading an insurrection in Bolivia. He was born in Rosario, Argentina, on June 14, 1928 to an impoverished upper-class family. His father was a failure both as an architect and as a businessman. Guevara suffered from chronic asthma from an early age, and his strong-willed mother doted on him. At 24 he received a medical degree, but by this time he wanted to become a revolutionary rather than a physician. His first political involvement was in his support for the left-wing government of Jacobo Arbenz Guzmán in Guatemala. The overthrow of this government by a CIA-sponsored coup in 1954 made him a lifelong enemy of the United States. After expulsion from Guatemala, Guevara met Fidel and Raul Castro in Mexico, and he became one of the original band of revolutionaries to land in Cuba in 1956. His military abilities soon became apparent, and Fidel Castro made him a military commander. Although Guevara was recognized as one of the heroes of the Cuban Revolution, he was suspicious and resentful of the Cuban Communists and their Soviet sponsors, which served to isolate him from power in Cuba. In 1960, he wrote his manual of revolution, *Guerilla War,* which was based on cultivating the support of the people; terrorism was to be avoided as counterproductive. After leaving Cuba, Guevara tried to export his brand of revolution to Latin America. He was killed in

Bolivia in 1967 while leading guerilla operations. It was his death and the resulting Guevara cult that has long served as a model for left-wing terrorists.

Abimael Guzmán (Peru)

Guzmán is the founder and current leader of the Peruvian terrorist organization, the Shining Path (Sendero Luminoso). He was born in 1934 into a middle-class Peruvian family. After receiving a Ph.D. in philosophy and a law degree from San Agustín National University in Arequipa, he became a professor of philosophy at the University of Huamanga in Ayacucho. He is married to Augusta La Torre. His interest in radical politics caused him to join the Communist Party of Peru (PCP) in the late 1950s. In 1964, Guzmán broke with the PCP and joined the Bandera Roja, a Maoist group. His stay with this group lasted until 1970 when it expelled him and his adherents for doctrinal heresy. Guzmán took this opportunity to start the Maoist rural guerrilla group Sendero Luminoso. He used his position as the personnel director of the University of Huamanga to recruit a cadre of leaders and student followers. Recruitment of local Indians soon followed, but it was not until 1980 that the Shining Path began a campaign of terror in rural areas. Guzmán has kept a low personal profile by operating through a national Directorate and a Central Committee, but a cult of personality has been used to motivate the movement. His nom de guerre is Comrade Gonzalo, and it is by this name that the Indian communities of the altiplano follow him. He rejects all compromises with other terrorist organizations and eschews contact with international terrorist groups. Devoted to Maoist principles, he hopes to expand the Shining Path's operations to other South American countries. The success of the Shining Path remains uncertain, but it has conducted one of the most violent terrorist campaigns in history.

George Habash (Palestine)

Habash has led the PFLP since he founded it in October 1977. He was born in Lod, Palestine, in 1926 of well-to-do Greek Orthodox parents. His family fled Lod in 1948 before the Jewish occupation. After receiving his medical degree from the American University of Beirut, Habash ran a medical clinic in Amman, Jordan. Jordan expelled Habash in 1957 as a possible intelligence agent for Syria. He then lived in Damascus until the split between Syria and Egypt caused him to move to a more secure base in Lebanon. In 1959, he founded the Arab Nationalists Movement (ANM) and launched himself into the politics of the Palestinians. In 1967, the PFLP was formed out of the ANM and three other organizations with Habash as its head. His group soon specialized in attacks on Israeli civilian airliners and Israeli citizens in neutral countries. Habash allied the PFLP with the PLO, but his practices have sometimes gone counter to PLO policy. He forged an alliance with the Japanese Red Army in the early 1970s. In recent years, Habash has attempted to reduce the conflicts between the PFLP and the PLO leadership. He has also maintained a lower profile in the terrorist community. At one time the Soviets favored Habash over Arafat in giving financial and military support, but they soon realized that he was unmanageable, and such support dropped off sharply. Since the early 1970s, Habash has gained most of his support from the Chinese. In recent years, Habash has developed a better working relationship with Arafat, and he has become one of the mainstays of the PLO.

Meir Kahane (United States)

Kahane was the founder and leader of the Jewish terrorist organization, the Jewish Defense League (JDL). An orthodox rabbi from New York City, he wanted revenge for past acts against Jews. His initial policy was to attack the enemies of Israel with campaigns of harassment. Soon this harassment turned violent, with JDL members engaging in terrorist acts against the Soviet Union and Middle Eastern countries. Since Kahane vocally supported these acts, U.S. legal authorities initiated court proceedings against him. Kahane decided to emigrate to Israel in 1971. In Israel, he became the leader of a militant Zionist organization, but his actions toward the Palestinians made Israeli officials uncomfortable, and he was arrested more than 100 times. Still, he became a popular political figure in Israel. An Egyptian-born air conditioner repairman assassinated Kahane in New York while he was on a speaking campaign in November 1990. His death percipitated several riots in Israel.

Leila Ali Khaled (Palestine)

Khaled is one of the most famous terrorists alive. She gained most of her fame as an aircraft hijacker during the Palestinian hijacking campaign in the late 1960s and early 1970s. Khaled was born in 1944 in Haifa, Palestine, but she became a refugee in 1948 when her family fled to Tyre, Lebanon. After attending the American University in Beirut and teaching school in Kuwait, she joined the PFLP soon after the outbreak of the 1967 Arab-Israeli War. Her participation in two big airline hijackings (TWA Flight 840 in August 1969 and El Al Flight 291 in September 1970) gained her international notoriety. Her accessibility to the press and her strong viewpoints made her a strong spokesperson for the Palestinian cause. Khaled's new infamy made her useless for further terrorist activity, however, and she has not been in the public eye since these actions, except for the publication of her memoirs. Some resentment of her high status as a terrorist figure has surfaced among the PFLP bureaucracy.

Sean MacStiofain (Northern Ireland)

MacStiofain was one of the major leaders of the Irish Republican Army Provisional Wing (IRA-Provos) in its early terrorist phase. He was born John Stephenson in London in February 1928, and his father was a Protestant law clerk with aristocratic pretensions who was also a violent alcoholic. At the age of nine, the young Stephenson was placed in a parochial school where he was instructed in Catholicism. Stephenson ran away from his father at age 14 and joined some Irish insurgents in London who were working for the reunification of Ireland. He stayed in this environment for several years and in 1950 he married an Irish-woman. Together with Cathal Goulding, he raided an armory to gain weapons for operations in Ulster, but they were captured and sentenced to eight years in jail at the Wormwood Scrubbs Prison. It was in jail that Stephenson changed his name to Sean MacStiofain and began to learn terrorist techniques from Greek Cypriot inmates. After his release from prison, MacStiofain became a leader in the IRA campaign in Ulster. He was one of the leaders in the split within the IRA between the Officials and the Provisionals in the early 1970s. MacStiofain became the chief of staff of the Provisionals and under his direction a terrorist campaign was launched against the Protestants in Ulster. The Republic of Ireland arrested him in November 1972 and sentenced him to six months in jail. He promised a hunger strike, but his inability to carry it out discredited him to his comrades in the Provos. By the spring of 1974, MacStiofain no longer had a leadership role in the IRA-Provos, and he was succeeded as chief of staff by Seamus Twomey. While MacStiofain still professes support for the Irish cause, he has been in permanent retirement since the 1970s.

Robert Jay Mathews (United States)

Mathews was the leader of the American right-wing racist terrorist group the Silent Brotherhood (also called The Order). He was born

in Marfa, Texas, on January 16, 1953. His father was a local businessman and the former mayor of Marfa before business conditions made
him move his family to Phoenix, Arizona, in 1958. As a boy, Mathews
was attracted to Robert Welch's John Birch Society and Robert Bolivar
DePugh's Minutemen. After failing to graduate from high school over
an economics course argument with a teacher, he formed a paramilitary organization of conservative Mormons and survivalists, the Sons
of Liberty. A falling out among the members of this group caused
Mathews to move to the Pacific Northwest where he met with the racist
religious leader Richard Butler. It was not until 1983 that Mathews
became more active in a leadership role in the racist right. He
founded the Silent Brotherhood in early 1984 to start a war with what
he termed the Zionist Occupation Government (ZOG). His group
started with counterfeiting and small-scale robberies to finance its
white supremacist cause, but soon Mathews was able to attract more
followers to his camp in northern Idaho. He also became more
ambitious and planned the assassination of the Jewish radio talk show
host, Alan Berg. After the Berg killing, he followed with the robbery
of a Brinks truck, which gave the Silent Brotherhood $3.8 million.
Mathews was busy planning more activities when the FBI closed in on
him. The FBI and police ambushed a house on Whidbey Island,
Washington, where Mathews died in the shootout. All of his followers
were rounded up, and most are serving long terms in federal prisons.

Carlos Marighella (Brazil)

Marighella split with the Brazilian Communist Party to become one
of the main theorists for terrorism. He was the son of an Italian
immigrant and a black Brazilian woman. In 1928 at the age of 16, he
joined the Brazilian Communist Party, an allegiance that lasted until
1967 when he founded the terrorist group Action for National Liberation (ALN). For nearly two years, Marighella acted as the head of
these urban guerrillas. He gathered the lessons from this experience
to write the chapter "Handbook of Urban Guerrilla Warfare," from
his book *For the Liberation of Brazil,* a work that became the textbook
for terrorists worldwide. His theory held that it was necessary for the
revolutionist to abandon party politics in favor of "armed insurrection
of the people." Marighella believed that the urban guerrilla had the
advantage over the forces of the state because the guerrilla defended
the cause of the people. In contrast, the military and the police were
always at a disadvantage, despite their superior military arms, because
they supported the status quo. He also advocated robbing banks as a

way to finance the revolution and kidnappings as a method to gain media attention. Marighella was killed in a police ambush organized by a right-wing death squad in São Paulo on November 4, 1969. His activities had become so threatening that the Brazilian government had launched a police crackdown on terrorist activity in Brazil. Despite his apparent lack of success, his handbook has been published in most European and Middle-Eastern languages, and his memory is still treated with reverence.

Ulrike Meinhof (West Germany)

Meinhof was a leader of the Red Army Faction. Born on October 7, 1934, in Oldenburg, Germany, her parents died when she was still young. Renate Riemeck, a historian and co-founder of the German Peace Union (DFU), acted as her guardian and political mentor. Her early education was in Catholic schools, and she majored in sociology and philosophy in Munich. An early political interest was an involvement as a student in the nuclear disarmament movement. She married Klaus Reiner Roehl, the publisher and editor of the popular journal, *Konkret,* for which she wrote a leftist column. In 1965, Meinhof had surgery on a brain tumor, after which she turned to radical politics. After leaving her husband, she joined the radical underground and became friends with Gudrun Ensslin, helping to release Ensslin's boyfriend, Andreas Baader (see related entries), from prison. She soon became one of the principal leaders of the Red Army Faction. For almost a year Meinhof participated in bombings and other attacks on the West German state in an attempt to destabilize it. Her terrorist activities made her a prime target of the police, and she was arrested in June 1972. In her trial in November 1974, she was sentenced to eight years in prison for her May 1970 rescue of Baader. After fellow terrorists made two unsuccessful attempts to free her in 1975, she was found hanging in her jail cell in the maximum-security Stammheim Prison in May 1976, an apparent suicide. A political uproar followed.

Abu Nidal (Sadri al-Banna) (Palestine)

The leader of the Abu Nidal Group of Palestinian terrorists was born Sadri al-Banna in 1937 at Jaffa, Palestine, of a wealthy Palestinian family. The family fled to Nablus in the Hashemite Kingdom of Transjordan in 1949, where he went to high school before enrolling at the University of Cairo to study engineering. After two years of study, Nidal worked as an electrician in Saudi Arabia during 1960–1962. It was here that Nidal first became involved in politics. He first joined the Ba'ath Party and then al-Fatah. Because of his political activities, he was fired from his job, tortured, and expelled from Saudi Arabia. Many of his anti-Saudi biases come from this experience. The 1967 war increased his involvement with al-Fatah. He became a close friend of one of Yasser Arafat's chief aides, Abu Iyad. After a period of service in the Sudan, he was sent to Iraq as the official PLO delegate. In Iraq, Nidal became so closely attached to the Iraqi intelligence services that he broke with al-Fatah's leadership. Since his break with al-Fatah and the PLO, Nidal has continued to promote internationalizing the Palestinian conflict even after other Palestinian organizations have renounced this tactic. He founded a violent rejectionist group named for him, which waged open warfare with PLO leaders. According to some estimates, several hundred PLO leaders have been assassinated by order of Abu Nidal. He is under a death sentence from the PLO, but this has done little to curtail his activities. Rumors have reached the outside world that Nidal is suffering from a heart condition and underwent heart operations in 1977, 1984, and 1986. News reports maintain that Qaddafi cut off funding for the Abu Nidal Group in 1989, and speculation is that Nidal and his followers are operating out of the Bekaa Valley in Lebanon.

Muammar El Qaddafi (Libya)

President Qaddafi of Libya has been one of the prime sponsors of terrorism in the Middle East. Qaddafi was born in 1942 to a poor Bedouin family (Qaddadfa). He attended primary school in Sirte and secondary school in Sebha, where he became an avid supporter of Gamal Abdul Nasser of Egypt. His political activity led to his expulsion from school in Fezzan. In 1963, he entered a military college at the Royal Libyan Military Academy in Benghazi where he was an indifferent military student. He again became involved in political agitation, this time leading secret revolutionary activities with other army officers in the Free Unitary Officers. He became head of Libya after a military coup in September 1969. Once in firm political control of Libya, Qaddafi was active in supporting wars of national liberation much as his hero Nasser had sponsored. A staunch enemy of Israel, Qaddafi opposes any compromise with Israel, seeing this as a betrayal of the Arab cause. His political beliefs have been published in an ideological treatise, the *Green Book,* in which he dismisses Western and Soviet institutions and replaces them with a new theory of Islamic society. He has been active in funding Palestinian terrorist organizations, but he has also feuded with them over strategy and tactics. His backing of other terrorist organizations in Northern Ireland and Central America has been constant. The 1986 brush with U.S. forces in Libya has toned down Qaddafi's public terrorism, but he is still one of the leading active supporters of terrorism.

Jean-Marc Rouillan (France)

Rouillan has been the leader of the French left-wing terrorist group Action Directe since its founding in 1979. He was born in 1953 in the French provincial town of Auch. While a student at the University of Toulouse in the early 1970s, Rouillan became active in the anti-Franco movement, joining the International Revolutionary Action Groups in 1974. His activities resulted in arrest by the French police in 1974 and again in 1978. It was in 1979 that Rouillan and his girlfriend, Nathalie Menignon, and others formed the terrorist group Action Directe. After a bank robbery and a raid for identity papers at a French government office, Rouillan was arrested in September 1980 by the French police. President Mitterrand's political amnesty in 1981 freed Rouillan from a stiff jail sentence. After Rouillan resumed his leadership role in Action Directe, he negotiated an unofficial alliance with Palestinian terrorists, launching a bombing campaign against Jewish targets in Paris. The French Government responded by outlawing Action Directe in August 1982. This banning only caused Rouillan to renew Action Directe's terrorist campaign and seek more allies among European terrorist groups. Rouillan, along with three other leaders, was arrested by French security forces in February 1987. His career as one of the leaders of Western Europe's terrorist alliance ended when he was sentenced to a long prison term.

Ali Hassan Salameh (Palestine)

Salameh, whose code name was the Red Prince, was one of the principal leaders of the Black September terrorist group and a close friend of the head of the PLO, Yasser Arafat (see entry). He was born in the spring of 1941 in Iraq. His father was a military chief and a devoted follower of the Mufti of Jerusalem, Haj Amin el Husseini, and was killed in the 1948 War leading Palestinian forces against the Israelis. Salameh grew up in a well-to-do suburb of Beirut, Lebanon, and his schooling was at Maqassed College and at Bir-Zeit (West Bank). Civil unrest in Beirut in 1958 caused the Salameh family to move to Cairo. Salameh was a good student and he studied engineering both in Egypt and in West Germany. It was at this time that he also gained a reputation as a playboy. In 1963 he returned to Cairo and married into the el Husseini family. Shortly after his marriage, he started work as a clerk in the PLO office in Kuwait. Salameh remained in this position until the Six Day War, when he joined al-Fatah. After some training by Egyptian intelligence services, Salameh became the Chief of Operations for Black September. He masterminded the attacks against Jordanian targets, and in September 1972, he planned the attack on the Israeli Olympic team in Munich. After Black September was disbanded at the end of 1973, Salameh became the head of al-Fatah's security and intelligence department. He was recognized by others in al-Fatah and the PLO as indispensable to Arafat. His marriage to Lebanese beauty queen Georgina Rizak only made him more visible in the terrorist world. On January 22, 1979, Salameh was assassinated by a Israeli car bomb in west Beirut. His death was mourned by thousands in Beirut.

Illich Ramirez Sanchez (Carlos) (Venezuela)

Sanchez, whose code name is Carlos, is one of the most feared terrorists still alive. He was born in Venezuela on October 12, 1949 and was raised by his lawyer father and socialite mother. His father had long held Communist sympathies; each of his three sons were named for Communist heroes. At the early age of 14, Sanchez started school at the Colegio Fermin Toro (1963–1966). After college, his father sent him to be educated in guerrilla tactics at Camp Mantanzas in Havana, Cuba, and then to the Soviet Union for a two-year course of study at the Patrice Lumumba University in Moscow. After completing this training, he conducted a series of terrorist operations that made the nom de guerre of Carlos world famous, peaking with the 1977 kidnapping of 11 Organization of Petroleum Exporting Countries (OPEC) ministers in Vienna. He became so famous that his career as an operative had to end. Most of his time since has been spent first in Libya training terrorists and then in Syria operating an anti-Iraqi network. In 1982, Carlos commanded Syrian hit teams assigned to wipe out President Assad's enemies in Europe. He is rumored to have married fellow terrorist, Magdalena Kaupp, in 1985. While Carlos is too notorious to conduct operations in person, his presence in many terrorist actions is still felt by Western counterterrorists. He is reputed to be the head of the Palestinian terrorist organization, the International Faction of Revolutionary Cells.

Oreste Scalzone (Italy)

Scalzone is famous as the leading theorist for the Italian Red Brigade. A former professor of politics and philosophy at the University of Padua, Scalzone has been charged with planning the Red Brigade's terrorist campaign. He was arrested in April 1979 in a mass roundup after the murder of Aldo Moro. After 17 months in jail, Scalzone was released on the grounds of ill health. Scalzone quickly fled to Paris, claiming political refugee status. In the intervening years, he has served as a theorist analyzing Italian terrorism. He now believes that terrorism has given the state in Italy and elsewhere the excuse to consolidate its power at the expense of political dissent. He also believes that the social and political reasons for terrorism in Italy are still present. The collapse of Red Brigade terrorism in Italy has reduced his stature in the terrorist world.

Raul Sendic (Uruguay)

Sendic is one of the founders and the leading figure in the Uruguayan terrorist organization, the Tupamaros. Little is known about his early life except that he was born in 1925 and quit law school to join the Socialist Party in the late 1950s. He ran for political office several times before retiring from the party to become active in grass-roots political agitation among sugar plantation workers. While he organized the Tupamaros movement in the early 1960s, it was not until activities shifted to Montevideo (where about half of the population of Uruguay lived) that the movement prospered. It thrived until the military instituted martial law in 1972 and the elected president was forced out of office in 1976. Sendic led the Tupamaros movement until his capture by the police sometime in 1972 or 1973. He was held in a maximum security prison at a military base until his release in 1985 as part of a general amnesty of political prisoners. He spent the next few years converting the Tupamaros into a legal political party. He died in April 1989 after suffering for years with ill health.

Yitzhak Shamir (Israel)

Shamir started his political career as one of the leaders of the most violent Jewish terror groups, the Stern Gang or the Lehi. Shamir was born in Poland under the name Yzernitzky. While in Poland, he became an adherent of the Irgun. He soon found the Irgun too moderate so he joined the breakaway faction led by charismatic Abraham Stern. Shamir became active in the violent terrorist campaign by the Stern Gang against the British in Palestine, eventually becoming one of its leaders after the death of Stern in 1942. Shamir has always defended the tactic of using personal terror through selective assassination and bombing, a policy that led to the revenge assassination of the former British colonial secretary, Lord Moyne, in 1944. Shamir was exiled by British authorities to Eritrea in 1946, but he soon surfaced in France where he was given political asylum. He returned to Israel in 1948. The Stern Gang's assassination of the UN mediator, Count Folke Bernadotte, in 1948 alienated many of their supporters. After the state of Israel was created, Shamir retired from politics until 1955. He held a senior position in the Civil Service until 1965, when business attracted him. It was not until 1970 that Shamir joined the Herut (Freedom) Movement. He was elected to the Knesset in 1973, and, after becoming influential in the nationalistic Likud (Unity) Party, he was elected speaker of the Knesset in 1977. Shamir has been Israeli prime minister twice (1983–1984) and (1986–1992), representing the policies of the Likud Party. His political fortune has mirrored the electoral fate of the Likud Party. Shamir has never displayed any remorse about his terrorist past.

Fusako Shigenobu (Japan)

Shigenobu is the acknowledged leader of the Japanese Red Army. She was born in Tokyo in 1945 into a family of shopkeepers. Her father was a former member of the right-wing Blood Oath League. Her family could not afford to send her to college. She married a left-wing radical, Tsnyoshi Okudaira, and for a short period she worked as a topless dancer in the Ginza district in Tokyo. Her husband was a leader in the Japanese Red Army until he killed himself during a terrorist attack on the Lod Airport in 1972. She soon assumed her place as one of the leaders of the JRA. Under her leadership the Japanese Red Army earned a reputation as one of the most violent terrorist organizations during the 1970s. Members were trained in terrorist tactics in the Middle East, and they established a close working relationship with the PFLP, even to the point of helping them with missions in the Middle East. Rumors circulated that the head of the PFLP, George Habash, and Shigenobu had become lovers. Internal purges, losses during terrorist operations, and difficulties recruiting new members always made the Japanese Red Army a small group. In the mid-1980s, Shigenobu announced in a news dispatch that the JRA was renouncing terrorist tactics, and most of its operations have since ceased. While Shigenobu is still wanted for her terrorist past, she has maintained a low profile since the announcement.

4

Selected Documents

MOST OFFICIAL DOCUMENTS on terrorism concern efforts to eradicate terrorism on an international scale. Early on, the reluctance of the United Nations and individual countries to unite against terrorism retarded antiterrorism agreements. It was only in the late 1970s, when terrorism appeared completely out of control, that nations signed joint agreements to fight it. Efforts taken by individual states proved to be ineffective, and only bilateral and multilateral agreements have effectively impeded international terrorism. The agreements listed in this chapter are only a few of the many negotiated treaties and agreements concluded to control international terrorism, but they give a representative picture of these attempts by Western states.

Both official documents from terrorist organizations and personal statements from terrorists give insight into their justifications for terrorism. The documents presented in this chapter are a reflection of these justifications, but they constitute only a sampling of the documents and writings available. The following are key documents in any study of terrorism.

The Palestinian National Charter

The basis for the terrorist war against Israel is in the Palestine Liberation Organization's (PLO) The Palestinian National Charter, revised in July 1968. An excerpt gives the PLO's stance on the use of terrorism:

> *Article 1:* Palestine, the homeland of the Palestinian Arab people, is an inseparable part of the greater Arab homeland, and the Palestinian people are a part of the Arab Nation.

Article 2: Palestine, within the frontiers it had during the British mandate, is an indivisible territorial unit.

Article 4: The Palestinian identity is an authentic, intrinsic and indissoluble quality that is transmitted from father to son. Neither the Zionist occupation nor the dispersal of the Palestinian Arab people as a result of the afflictions they have suffered can efface this Palestinian identity.

Article 5: Palestinians are Arab citizens who were normally resident in Palestine until 1947. This includes both those who were forced to leave or who stayed in Palestine. Anyone born to a Palestinian father after that date, whether inside or outside Palestine, is Palestinian.

Article 6: Jews who were normally resident in Palestine up to the beginning of the Zionist invasion are Palestinians.

Article 8: The Palestinian people is[*sic*] at the stage of national struggle for the liberation of its homeland. For that reason, differences between Palestinian national forces must give way to the fundamental difference that exists between Zionism and imperialism on the one hand, and the Palestinian Arab people on the other....

Article 9: Armed struggle is the only way to liberate Palestine, and is thus strategic, not tactical. The Palestinian Arab people hereby affirm their unwavering determination to carry on the armed struggle and to press on toward popular revolution for the liberation of and return of their homeland....

Article 10: Commando action constitutes the nucleus of the Palestinian popular liberation war....

Article 12: The Palestinian people believe in Arab unity....

Article 15: The liberation of Palestine is a national obligation for Arabs. It is their duty to repel the Zionist and imperialist invasion of the greater Arab homeland and to liquidate the Zionist presence in Palestine....

Article 19: The partition of Palestine, which took place in 1947, and the establishment of the state of Israel, are fundamentally invalid, however long they last, for they contravene the will of the people of Palestine and their natural right to their homeland and contradict the principles of the United Nations Charter, foremost among which is the right of self-determination.

Article 20: The Balfour Declaration, the Mandate Instrument, and all their consequences, are hereby declared null and void. The claim of historical or spiritual links between the Jews and Palestine is neither in conformity with historical fact nor does it satisfy the requirements for statehood. Judaism is a revealed religion; it is not a separate nationality nor are the Jews a single people with a separate identity; they are citizens of their respective countries.

Article 21: The Palestinian Arab People, expressing themselves through the Palestinian armed revolution, reject all alternatives to the total liberation of Palestine....

Article 22: Zionism is a political movement that is organically linked to world imperialism and is opposed to all liberation movements or movements for progress in the world. The Zionist movement is essentially fanatical and racialist; its objectives involve aggression, expansion and the establishment of colonial settlements and its methods are those of the Fascists and the Nazis....

Article 27: The Palestine Liberation Organization shall cooperate with all Arab countries, each according to its means, maintaining a neutral attitude vis-a-vis these countries in accordance with the requirements of the battle of liberation, and on the basis of that factor. The Organization shall not interfere in the internal affairs of any Arab state.

Source: Charles L. Geddes, ed., *A Documentary History of the Arab-Israeli Conflict* (New York: Praeger, 1991), 137–142.

Extradition Agreement between the United States and Cuba, February 1973

A breakthrough that ended regular aircraft hijacking by Cubans and anti-Castro terrorists in the late 1960s and early 1970s was the February 1973 agreement between the United States and Cuba. Aircraft were hijacked frequently, almost weekly, and flown to Cuba or the United States. Both governments soon became concerned about these hijackings. This agreement contained provisions to return hijackers and aircraft to the jurisdiction of the crime, along with setting punishment for the offense. Despite some threats to abrogate this agreement on the part of Cuba, it is still in force.

1. Memorandum of Understanding on Hijacking of Aircraft and Vessels and Other Offenses

The Government of the United States of America and the Government of the Republic of Cuba, on the bases of equality and strict reciprocity, agree:

First: Any person who hereafter seizes, removes, appropriates or diverts from its normal route or activities an aircraft or vessel registered under the laws of one of the parties and brings it to the territory of the other party shall be considered to have committed an offense and therefore shall either be returned to the party of the registry of the aircraft or vessel to be tried by the courts of that party in conformity with its laws or be brought before the courts of the party whose territory he reached for trial in conformity with its laws for the offense punishable by the most severe penalty according to the circumstances and the seriousness of the acts to which this Article refers. In addition, the party whose territory is reached by the aircraft or vessel shall take all necessary steps to facilitate without delay the continuation of the journey of the passengers and crew innocent of the hijacking....

Second: Each party shall try with a view to severe punishment in accordance with its laws any person who, within its territory, hereafter conspires to promote, or promotes, or prepares, or directs, or forms part of an expedition which from its territory or any other place carries out acts of violence or depredation against aircraft or vessels....

Third: Each party shall apply strictly its own laws to any national of the other party who, coming from the territory of the other party, enters its territory, violating its laws as well as national and international requirements pertaining to immigration, health, customs and the like.

Fourth: The party in whose territory the perpetrators of the acts described in Article First arrive may take into consideration any extenuating or mitigating circumstances in those cases in which the persons responsible for the acts were being sought for strictly political reasons and were in real and imminent danger of death without a viable alternative for leaving the country, provided there was no financial extortion or physical injury to the members of the crew, passengers, or other persons in connection with the hijacking.

Source: Robert A. Friedlander, *Terrorism: Documents of International and Local Control,* vol. 2 (Dobbs Ferry, NY: Oceana, 1979), 137–139.

World View of a Member of the Red Army Faction

The most violent social revolutionaries have been the Red Army Faction (RAF), or as it was sometimes called the Baader-Meinhof Gang, operating in former West Germany. This group intended to destabilize the West German state to provoke the masses into accepting social revolution. RAF member Holger Meins wrote this letter to his friend Manfred Grashof on 31 October 1974, shortly before he died during a hunger strike. It expresses much of the world view and motivation of the RAF members.

Either human being or pig. The only thing that matters is the struggle now, today, tomorrow—whether we eat or not. What is important is what you make out of it. A leap forward to become better, to learn from experience. The point is that one has to learn from all of this. Everything else is dirt. The struggle will continue. Every new fight, every action, every skirmish, brings with it new unknown experiences, and that is the evolution of the struggle. It can only evolve in this manner—the subjective side of the dialectic of revolution and counterrevolution. What is decisive is to understand how to learn.

Through the struggle, for the struggle; from the victories, but even more from the mistakes, from the knockdowns, from the defeats. That is the law of Marxism.

To fight, to be defeated, once more to fight, to be defeated again, to fight anew and so on and on to the final victory. That is the logic of the people says the old man.

Man is nothing but matter, as is everything else. The whole human being, body and consciousness, is material matter, and what makes a human being what he is; his freedom is that his consciousness rules over matter, over itself and over external nature and, above all, over one's own existence. The one side of Engels, crystal clear; the guerrilla, however, materializes himself in the struggle, in the revolutionary action, and that means without an end; that is, fight to the death, and, of course, collectively.

That is no concern for matter but one for politics. Of practice. As you say, concern is always today, tomorrow, and onward. Yesterday has been. Criterion also but above all concern. Whatever now rests first of all with you. The HS [Hit Song] has a long way to go yet before it ends.

And the fight will never end.

But there is, of course, a point to be made. If you know that with every pig victory, the concrete intention to commit murder becomes more concrete and you then decide to pull out, to have more safety for yourself, and by this action give victory to the pigs—that is, you desert us—then you are the pig that splits and withdraws in order to survive yourself. Then you just keep your mouth shut. Don't say something like the Practiced Slogan: "Long live the RAF. Death to the system of the pigs." When you no longer hunger with us, then you should have the guts—it would be more honest, if you still know the meaning of honor—to say "I live. Down with the RAF. Victory to the system of the pigs."

Either pig or human being
Either survival at any price or fight to the death
Either problems or solutions
In between there is nothing

Victory or death say our types everywhere, and that is the language of the guerrilla even in the tiny dimension here, because with life it is the same as with dying. Human beings, meaning us, who refuse to give up the struggle, they either win or they die, instead of losing and of dying.

Pretty sad to have to write you something like that. Of course, I don't know how that is either, when ones dies or when they kill one. Where should I know it from? In a moment of truth one morning it penetrated my skull as the very first thought: So it is going to be that way. Certainly had not known it yet and then right in front of the barrel aimed right between the eyes—well, anyway, that was it. In any case, on the right side.

I'll tell you this, man: Everyone dies anyway. What matters is how, and how you lived. It's simple. Fighting the pigs as a human being for the liberation of man, as a revolutionary, fighting to the last, loving life, disdaining death. That's my idea of serving the people and the RAF.

Source: Ovid Demaris, *Brothers in Blood: The International Terrorist Network* (New York: Scribner's, 1977), 248–249.

Relationship of the Soviet Union and the PLO

The relationship between the former Soviet Union and the PLO has been characterized as one between sponsor and client, but this claim is far too simplistic. Evidence is available that Soviet authorities asked the PLO for advice and were willing to defer to their wishes on matters of policy and tactics. Most U.S. experts interpreted the relationship as more one-sided with the Soviets masterminding it. An Israeli operation in the PLO headquarters in Sidon, Lebanon, uncovered the following transcript of a conversation between Andre Gromyko, the Soviet foreign minister, and Yasser Arafat, the head of the PLO, on November 13, 1979.

> *Gromyko:* First of all, I will speak of the main problems of international politics, and about our position concerning these problems.
>
> The USSR continues its principle policy regarding the Middle East as it did in the past. We are in favor of Israel's withdrawal from the occupied territories and in favor of granting the Palestinians their legitimate rights and the establishment of their independent state, together with the right of all states in the region to be sovereign. This is the essence of our position regarding problems of the Middle East....
>
> We are now just prior to the presentation of the Palestinian issue in the UN. This matter is very important to us and to yourselves. We will no doubt support and assist the Palestinian and Arab position, and we will back every proposal and every plan that you submit to the UN. This support also applies to our socialist comrades. The last question is, and it is only a question: it is known that America—when it talks with us about the Palestinian problem—its delegates tell us: how is it possible for us to recognize the PLO and the establishment of an independent Palestinian state when the PLO does not recognize Israel?
>
> Are you considering certain tactical concessions in return for getting recognition from the hostile camp? And are you also considering recognizing Israel's right to exist as an independent sovereign state?

During the discussions with the Americans, we felt we were at a dead end. Here I would like to know what your opinion is and please regard it as a question only....

Arafat: Knowing that we are the victim, we raised many possible solutions, while none of our enemies presented any. We said: A democratic state where Jews and Arabs will live. They said: This means the destruction of Israel. In 1974, we said we will establish the Palestinian state on every part of land that Israel withdraws from, or which will be liberated, and this is our right.

We have proposed all these things and they have offered nothing.

Gromyko: If there is a change in your position, I ask you to notify us, since one cannot escape this issue. In every statement, the Americans say: How can we recognize an organization while they are not ready to recognize anything? This is demagoguery, but we have to know how to deal with it. I ask you to think about it and make your comments.

I thank you for the useful discussion. We think that we march with you on the same path concerning the Middle East problem. The Soviet Union is a friend of the Arabs and does not tend to change its friends. We hope that the Arabs and the PLO feel the same way.

Arafat: The PLO has no doubts.

Source: James Adams, *The Financing of Terror: How the Groups That Are Terrorizing the World Get the Money to Do It* (New York: Simon and Schuster, 1986), 45–46.

PLO Guidelines for Attacking Civilian Targets in Israel

Among the documents captured by Israeli forces in 1982 was one that provided guidelines for PLO terrorist activities inside Israel. This document described target selection for maximum damage and publicity. The section on targeting the civilian population is the one included below.

Section 6
Target Selection and Timing of the Operations

1. The blow must be directed at the enemy's weak point. His greatest weakness is his small population. Therefore, operations must be launched which will liquidate immigration into Israel. This can be achieved by various means: attacking absorption centers for new immigrants; creating problems for them in their new homes by sabotaging their water and electricity supply; using weapons in terrifying ways against them where they live, and using arson whenever possible.

2. Any installation which is designated as a target must meet the criterion of importance to the civilian population. Blows directed at secondary or isolated targets, whose impact passes unnoticed, are of no use.

3. Attacks can be made to multiply their impact. For instance, attacking a tourist installation during the height of the tourist season is much more useful than dealing the same blow at another time. If fuel tanks are set on fire during an energy crisis, this can be much more useful than at another time. Likewise, dealing a blow to the enemy immediately following his own attack constitutes an excellent reprisal which is beneficial to our morale.

4. Density of the population in the streets and market places of cities tends to increase on special occasions like holidays and vacations. One ought to bear this in mind in order to better select the place of action and improve the impact of the blow.

5. Attention should be given to the safety of our people. The type of action should take their safety into consideration.

Source: Raphael Israeli, ed., *PLO in Lebanon: Selected Documents* (London: Weidenfeld and Nicolson, 1983), 31.

Training of Terrorist Organizations

International terrorist rings depend on cooperation among terrorist groups for training. The following report gives an indication of the number of groups that trained in Lebanon during the early 1980s. This information came from an unidentified source in Turkey's Istanbul GUNES news service on July 17, 1982

It has been disclosed that militants belonging to 40 terrorist organizations from various countries received training in the past five years in the PLO (Palestine Liberation Organization) camps in Lebanon. It has been stated that among the foreign terrorists trained in these camps, Turkish terrorists top the list. According to information, the following are some of the organizations trained in the PLO camps:

Turkish: Dev-Sol (Revolutionary Left); Dev-Yol (Revolutionary Way); TKP-ML (Turkish Communist Party-Marxist-Leninist); TKIP (Turkish Communist Workers Party); Acilciler (The Swift Ones); Halkin Devirimci Conculeri (People's Revolutionary Pioneers); Dev-Savas (Revolutionary Fight); MLSPB (Marxist-Leninist Armed Propaganda Union [or Unit]); Devirimci Halk Birligi (Revolutionary Turkish People's Union); Tukiye Devrimci Kommunist Partisi (Turkish Revolutionary Communist Party); Apolcular (Followers of the Abdyllah Ocal Group).

European: Red Brigades; ETA (Basque Nation and Liberty); IRA (Irish Republican Army); RAF (German Red Army Faction); the Italian Marxist-Leninist Vanguard Organization; the Corsican Separatists; the Swiss Anarchists Union.

United States, Asian and Africans: The Secret Army for the Liberation of Armenia (ASALA); the Japanese Red Army; the National Liberation Front of El Salvador; the Nicaraguan Sandinista guerrillas; the Argentine Montoneros guerrillas; the Peronist Revolutionary Movement; the American Indian Movement; Sri Lanka guerrillas; the Ku Klux Klan; the Dhofar Front guerrillas.

The WSG, known as the War Sports Group, representing the neo-Nazis, is also reported to have received training in the PLO camps. It is reported that these militants, who have embarked on various acts of militancy against foreign workers in Germany, particularly against Turkish workers, are among those trained in the PLO camps. In the past few months, two Turkish workers were killed by members of this organization.

Source: Edward F. Mickolus, Todd Sandler, and Jean M. Murdock, *International Terrorism in the 1980s: A Chronology of Events* (Ames: Iowa State University Press, 1989), 296.

Venice Statement on Terrorism, June 9, 1987

The prolonged campaign against international terrorism culminated in a series of statements by the seven industrialized powers at Bonn, Ottawa, London, Tokyo, and Venice. The Venice statement is included to give the flavor of these statements.

Terrorism

We the heads of state or government of seven major democracies and the representatives of the European Community assembled here in Venice, profoundly aware of our peoples' concern at the threat posed by terrorism:

Reaffirm our commitment to the statements on terrorism made at previous summits, in Bonn, Venice, Ottawa, London and Tokyo;

Resolutely condemn all forms of terrorism, including aircraft hijackings and hostage-taking, and reiterate our belief that whatever its motives, terrorism has no justification;

Confirm the commitment of each of us to the principle of making no concessions to terrorists or their sponsors;

Remain resolved to apply, in respect of any state clearly involved in sponsoring or supporting international terrorism, effective measures within the framework of international law and in our own jurisdictions;

Welcome the progress made in international cooperation against terrorism since we last met in Tokyo in May 1986, and in particular the initiative taken by France and Germany to convene in May in Paris a meeting of the ministers of nine countries, who are responsible for counterterrorism;

Reaffirm our determination to combat terrorism both through national measures and through international cooperation among ourselves and with others, when appropriate, and therefore renew our appeal to all like-minded countries to consolidate and extend international cooperation in all appropriate fora;

Will continue our efforts to improve the safety of travelers. We welcome improvements in airport and maritime security, and encourage the work of I.C.A.O. and I.M.O. in this regard. Each of us will continue to monitor closely the activities of airlines which raise security problems. The heads of state or government have decided on measures, annexed to this statement, to make the 1978 Bonn Declaration more effective in dealing with all forms of terrorism affecting civil aviation;

Commit ourselves to support the rule of law in bringing terrorists to justice. Each of us pledges increased cooperation in the relevant fora and within the framework of domestic and international law on the investigation, apprehension and prosecution of terrorists. In particular we reaffirm the principle established by relevant international conventions of trying and extraditing, according to national laws and those international conventions, those who have perpetrated acts of terrorism.

Annex

The heads of state or government recall that in their Tokyo statement on international terrorism they agreed to make the 1978 Bonn Declaration more effective in dealing with all forms of terrorism affecting civil aviation. To this end, in cases where a country refuses extradition or prosecution of those who have committed offenses described in the Montreal Convention for the Suppression of Unlawful Acts against the Safety of Civil Aviation and/or does not return the aircraft involved, the heads of state or government are jointly resolved that their Governments shall take immediate action to cease flights to that country as stated in the Bonn Declaration.

At the same time, their governments will initiate action to halt incoming flights from that country or from any country by the airlines of the country concerned as stated in the Bonn Declaration.

The heads of state or government intend also to extend the Bonn declaration in due time to cover any future relevant amendment to the above convention or any other aviation conventions relating to the extradition or prosecution of the offenders.

The heads of state or government urge other governments to join them in this commitment.

Source: U.S. House of Representatives, Committee on Foreign Affairs, *International Terrorism: A Compilation of Major Laws, Treaties, Agreements, and Executive Documents* (Washington, DC: U.S. Government Printing Office, 1987), 207.

5

Directory of Terrorist Organizations, 1940–1992

TERRORIST ORGANIZATIONS HAVE a short life expectancy. Once a group engages in terrorism, the full machinery of a state is usually directed toward its eradication. Some states are not efficient at stopping terrorism, and other states actually support terrorist groups, but sooner or later each terrorist organization faces opposition.

Internal dissension has caused more than one terrorist group to become ineffective. A common way for terrorist organizations to avoid internal fragmentation is to create separate political and military wings. In this way, one part of the organization can claim ignorance of the actions of the other, and there are more leadership positions available for the politically ambitious. This complexity, however, makes studying terrorist groups difficult. Sometimes the military wing of a terrorist organization goes by a completely different name and has a structure which is independent of its political counterpart.

Another common feature among terrorist organizations is fragmentation. Often, factions within a terrorist group opt to break away, and the new groups often adopt tactics, methods, and even names similar to those of the parent organizations. Because of personalities and tactical differences, open warfare has erupted on occasion between these previous allies. Fragmentation is the reason that as many as 500 terrorist groups may have existed since 1945.

It is impossible to determine the exact number of terrorist organizations because of the practice of terrorists to use dummy names for operations. The following list of 84 terrorist organizations is an attempt to bring coherence to a situation that is always in a state of flux. This selected list is arranged by the names of organizations most likely to be known by English-speaking readers. For more information on particular terrorists, consult the biographies in chapter 3; additional details about individual terrorist acts may be found in the chronology in chapter 2.

Abu Nidal Group or Palestinian National Liberation Movement (Syria)
The Abu Nidal Group, which also goes by the name of the Palestinian National Liberation Movement, is a Palestinian terrorist organization that was initially sponsored and supported with funds from Syria. It was formed in 1974 by the terrorist leader Sadri al-Banna, who calls himself Abu Nidal, to protest the involvement of Syrian forces in the Lebanese civil war. For a time, this group was called Black June.

Initial estimates were that this group had several hundred hard-core members organized into terrorist cells of three to seven people. A more recent assessment places this group with 500 members in Libya, and more than 2,000 members in Lebanon. Recruits for terrorist activities are gathered from Palestinian refugee camps in Lebanon. This group's original opposition to Syria has been mollified over time. It has received support from Syria (1983–1987) and Iraq (1973–1974), but most of this group's financial and moral backing now comes from Libya.

Abu Nidal conflicts violently with the Palestine Liberation Organization (PLO), and his group has carried out several assassination attempts against PLO leaders. An estimated 90 moderate PLO leaders and supporters have been eliminated by the Abu Nidal Group. He, in return, is under an al-Fatah death sentence. Several of the most bloody bombings and terrorist attacks have been conducted by members of this group and its intimidation of moderate Arabs has made a peaceful settlement of Israeli-Palestinian issues more difficult. After losing Qaddafi's financial support in 1989, this group has scaled down activities. Abu Nidal and most of his followers are reported to be operating out of the Bekaa Valley in Lebanon.

Action Directe [Direct Action] (AD) (France)
This small group of French left-wing terrorists with anarchist tendencies has been the most active terrorist organization in France. Jean-Marc

Rouillan and Nathalie Menignon founded this group in 1979. AD was constituted out of two smaller organizations: the International Revolutionary Action Group (GARI), an anti-Franco group, and the New Arms for Popular Autonomy (NAPAP), a Maoist group of urban guerrillas. French authorities declared this organization illegal in 1982 because of its ongoing terrorist activities.

AD is considered unique among European terrorist groups in that a high proportion of foreign citizens and women form its leadership cadre. Its members tend to be young and unemployed, but highly educated. Members have engaged in bombings, assassinations, and sabotage, especially sabotage that involves the destruction of computer facilities. The members have an anarchist desire to destroy French institutions and to kill key French and NATO political figures. Most of the leaders were arrested by French police in February 1987 and they are presently serving long prison terms. A lack of leadership and public indifference has made this group less active since 1987.

African National Congress (ANC) (South Africa)
The ANC, the oldest terrorist organization in existence, was founded in 1912 to fight against government restrictions directed toward the South African black population. It has a long history of attempting to work within the South African political system, but the Republic of South Africa's anti-apartheid program resulted in ANC's exclusion from parliamentary politics.

For many years, Chief Albert Luthuli was the moderate leader of the ANC. Only after decades of isolation did members of the ANC, under the leadership of Nelson Mandela and Oliver Tambo, resort to terrorism, avoiding civilian targets until the mid-1980s. Some of the more militant members of ANC started a widespread bombing campaign in 1984. ANC utilized bases in Mozambique, Botswana, and Zimbabwe to train members in guerrilla and terrorist warfare. At its peak, the ANC had around 6,000 guerrillas operating out of those countries.

The jailing of most of the ANC leaders over the years hurt its effectiveness, but international pressure concerning South African apartheid policies brought about reforms in the early 1990s. Nelson Mandela's release from prison in 1991 and the reforms of the DeKlerk government have made this party turn away from terrorism. While this organization is in transition from a terrorist to a significant political party in South Africa, violence still breaks out among its members and rival political organizations.

Amal (Lebanon)

The Amal is a Lebanese Shi'ite paramilitary organization founded by Moussa al-Sadr in 1975. This organization opposed PLO activities in Lebanon until the Immam disappeared on a visit to Libya in 1978. Leadership was then passed to Nabih Berri, who is a lawyer by training, and who has gradually led the Amal to adopt a more pro-PLO orientation. Members of the Amal are credited with developing the suicide bomb.

This organization became more active against Israel after the Israeli invasion of Lebanon in 1986. Many of the Shi'ite terrorist groups came out of the membership of this more moderate organization, and some of these terrorists still retain membership in the Amal. This group has had a high profile in negotiations with terrorist groups holding hostages, but has steadily lost membership to more active terrorist organizations. Much of Amal's influence in Beirut was lost to the Hezbollah, and open fighting between the two groups occurred until a formal truce was negotiated on January 30, 1989. Incidents still break out between the two groups, but open warfare no longer exists.

Arab National Youth Organization for the Liberation of Palestine (ANYOLP) (Libya)

This terrorist organization was founded by Libya's President Qaddafi in 1972, joining disaffected terrorists from Black September and the PFLP to carry out Qaddafi's wishes on the Palestinian question. Qaddafi selected as its leader Ahmed al-Ghaffour, a former Lebanese supporter of al-Fatah. The exact strength of this organization has always been unknown, but it has never been considered a major force among the Palestinian groups.

ANYOLP became active in terrorism at a time when the PLO was trying to win respectability with the world community, and most of its attacks were bloody. Since the execution of al-Ghaffour by the PLO as a traitor in 1973, this group has become less active. Qaddafi may not have formally disbanded it, but former members have moved to other organizations.

Argentine Anti-Communist Alliance or Triple A (Alianza Argentina Anti-Comunista) (Argentina)

Triple A was the leading right-wing counterterrorist organization in Argentina during the 1970s and early 1980s. It was founded by José Lopez Rega, who was the Minister for Social Welfare in Isabel Peron's last government. He ran the organization and its secret death squads from his ministry.

Charges have been made that Rega used state funds to buy weapons and to recruit members of the police for his organization. Kidnappings, torture, and murder were standard weapons used by the Triple A, which became a government institution after the military coup of General Videla in March 1976. Under powers granted to it by a state of siege, the government and its allies pursued a policy of extermination of perceived enemies. Only after the collapse of the military junta in 1983 did the Triple A lose its official status. Elements of the Triple A still exist, but so few witnesses remain that members have never been charged with crimes.

Armed Forces of National Liberation (Fuerzas Armadas de Liberacion Nacional) (FALN) (United States)

Formed in 1974 by American-born Puerto Ricans from two nationalist movements, the Armed Commandos of Liberation and the Armed Independence Revolutionary Movement, this Puerto Rican terrorist organization operates in the United States. Its goal is to liberate Puerto Rico from U.S. domination by the selective use of terror.

Carlos Alberto Torres is the acknowledged leader of the FALN, but he is serving a long prison term for his terrorist activities. Estimates place the group's strength at only about 50 active members, many of whom are serving long prison terms, but FALN does enjoy some support within the Puerto Rican community. It has staged about 200 bomb attacks, mostly in the New York City area, but some effort has been made to expand to Chicago.

An attempt to break the leaders out of a federal prison in 1986 was foiled by police. Adherents are still attracted to this organization, as the status of Puerto Rico remains uncertain, but it has not been as active in the early 1990s.

Armed Forces of National Liberation (Fuerzas Armadas de Liberacion Nacional) (FALN) (Venezuela)

The Venezuelan FALN was a revolutionary terrorist group formed in 1962 to overthrow the government of Venezuela. Most of its leadership came from the failed guerrilla group, the Movement of Left Revolutionaries (MIR), but it also had allies from the Communist Party and anti-government military officers. Fabricio Ojeda represented MIR and Douglas Bravo led the Communists.

The group initially concentrated its activities in rural areas, but eventually transferred its terrorist activities to Caracas. For a couple of years the FALN conducted a violent campaign, including assassinations, bombings, airliner hijackings, and kidnappings. Almost as suddenly as it started, the terrorist activity of the FALN ended when the terrorists actions were repudiated in a presidential election. The subsequent death of Ojeda in June 1966 ended the hope of a revival.

Armed Revolutionary Forces of Colombia (FARC) (Colombia)
This terrorist organization was formed in 1966 as the military wing of the Colombian Communist Party with the avowed goal of overthrowing the government and the ruling class. Manuel Marulanda Velez led this group, whose strength has been estimated at about 10,000 to 15,000 members and is primarily based in rural areas.

Despite its revolutionary goals, FARC did not become prominent until the mid-1970s, when its members went into the kidnap-for-ransom business. It became so prosperous that it began to offer protection for cocaine producers to raise more money. FARC is supposed to have levied a 10 percent protection payment on all coca growers in their territory. By the early 1980s, this organization had several thousand operatives involved in the drug traffic, perhaps controlling as much as 20 percent of all cocaine exports from Colombia.

Financial success has meant that FARC has become less active in terrorism. A truce with the Colombian government was negotiated in 1984 in which some of the terrorists reentered society and some FARC leaders assumed government posts.

Armed Revolutionary Nuclei (Nuclei Armati Rivoluzionari) (NAR) (Italy)
The Armed Revolutionary Nuclei (NAR) is the principal Italian right-wing terrorist group. Paolo Signorelli founded the NAR in 1979 to fight left-wing terrorism and to re-establish fascism in Italy. From the beginning the NAR has been closely linked with the neofascist student organization, the University Front for National Action (FUAN).

Estimates place the size of this group as not larger than 30 members, but it has engaged in several large-scale terrorist incidents. Among its active members have been several former high-ranking military officers. Its bombing of the Bologna railway station in August 1980 killed 84 people and wounded 189 others. This organization has maintained a less active profile since Italian police began a crackdown on left-wing terrorism and extended its attention to NAR.

Armenian Secret Army for the Liberation of Armenia (ASALA)
(Turkey)

Members of ASALA have conducted a terrorist campaign against Turkey in retaliation for Turkish massacres of Armenians in 1896 and 1915. This Marxist-Leninist organization was founded in 1975 in Beirut, Lebanon, and it has long had links to the pro-Syrian factions of the PLO.

Members of ASALA have attacked Turkish diplomats and property around the world. Between 1975 and 1982, 50 Turkish diplomats and staff were assassinated by members of the ASALA. Its goal is the establishment of an Armenian state out of portions of Turkey and the former Soviet Union. ASALA has been most active in France and the United States, particularly in California. Sporadic acts of terrorism are still carried out by this organization.

In 1983, a split developed between two factions within the ASALA, and the majority left to form a new group, the ASALA Revolutionary Movement (ASALA-RM). The more radical segments of ASALA formed the ASALA-M (Militant), and its leader was Hagop Hagopian until his assassination in Athens in May 1988. The leader of the more moderate ASALA-RM is Monte Melkonian.

Aryan Nation (AN) (United States)

This American right-wing terrorist group is also allied with the Church of Jesus Christ Christian. It was founded in 1974 by Richard Girnt Butler, with the goal of forming a whites-only nation in the Pacific Northwest of the United States. A computer bulletin board, called the Aryan Liberty Net of the Aryan Nations, has allowed the Aryan Nations to establish contact with other right-wing groups in North America.

In the early 1980s, Butler claimed 6,000 members in all 50 states and Canada, but a more realistic estimate of dedicated supporters is less than 1,000. It has also recruited members from the Aryan Brotherhood, a prison group espousing white supremacy. In the past, this group has held an annual summer convention in Hayden Lake, Idaho. Butler has been careful to avoid conflicts with the law, but several members of his group belong to other groups that have been engaged in terrorist activities, including bank and armored-car robberies. Some evidence exists that elements of the Aryan Nation have formed a working relationship with Louis Farrakhan's Nation of Islam to promote anti-Jewish propaganda.

Atonement and Holy Flight (al-Takfir Wal Higra) (Egypt)
This Islamic fundamentalist terrorist group aims to rid Egypt of secularism and to revive Islamic fundamentalism within the society. Some authorities estimate that this group has as many as 1,000 adherents, but its strength is in the large number of university students that are sympathetic to its cause.

Atonement and Holy Flight carried out terrorist acts against Coptic Christians until President Sadat cracked down by arresting many of the group's adherents. The leadership of this group retaliated by arranging the assassination of Anwar Sadat in 1981. Most followers disappeared after the assassination, but many of them have resurfaced in other Islamic fundamentalist groups.

Black Panther Party (BPP) (United States)
One of the outgrowths of the civil rights unrest of the 1960s was the Black Panthers. Although it originated as a local political party in Alabama, it gained most of its fame in Oakland, California. Early leaders were Bobby Seale and Huey Newton, but the writings of Eldridge Cleaver, particularly *Soul on Ice* (1968), assumed importance in the movement.

Beginning more as a self-defense group with a strong black nationalist bent, the Panthers soon became aggressive, facing off against the police in armed confrontations. Martin Luther King, Jr.'s assassination helped move the group toward the revolutionary left. The death of a policeman in October 1967 and the subsequent trial of Newton caused the party to reorient itself toward more legal means of action. Several former members of the BPP joined other groups involved in terrorist activities.

Black September (Palestine)
This group was formed in the aftermath of the repression of Palestinians in Jordan by King Hussein in September 1970. It served as the unofficial terrorist wing of al-Fatah, and its leader may have been Abu Iyad (Salah Khalef), a key figure in al-Fatah. Its chief of operations was Ali Hassan Salameh, who planned most of Black September's operations. Much of its financial support came from Libya, whose aid was estimated at more than $40 million by the mid-1970s, though disputes between al-Fatah and President Qaddafi dried up most of these funds.

While the majority of Black September's early activities were directed against Jordanian authorities (such as the assassination of Jordanian

Prime Minister Wasfi al-Tal), this group began to attack Israeli targets in 1972. At its peak, Black September had as many as 400 operatives with more potential recruits in al-Fatah. Its most famous terrorist act was the massacre of Israeli athletes at the Munich Olympic Games in September 1972. Black September maintained a low profile once the PLO initiated efforts to become more moderate, and it was disbanded in late 1973.

Central American Revolutionary Worker's Party (PRTC) (El Salvador)
The Central American Revolutionary Worker's Party (PRTC) is a Marxist-Leninist urban terrorist group operating mostly in El Salvador. It was formed in 1976 as part of a Central American regional insurgency operation. In 1980, the PRTC joined the umbrella group Frente Farabundo Marti de Liberacion Nacional (FMLN) to defeat the El Salvadoran army and its U.S. military advisers.

While this group is among the smallest in the FMLN, it has carried out some of the most violent terrorist attacks. Most of its targets have been U.S. businessmen and servicemen. Its strength has been estimated to be in the several hundreds, with many more sympathizers. Many of its members have also received military and terrorist training outside of El Salvador.

Countermeasures by the El Salvadoran military badly damaged the operative capabilities of this group after 1985, but it still constitutes a danger. Leaders of this group helped negotiate the peace settlement of January 1992, when a compromise between the government and the insurgents was concluded. Members of the PRTC were given an opportunity to abandon terrorism and return to civilian pursuits.

Cinchoneros Popular Liberation Movement (Honduras)
This left-wing terrorist organization became active in Honduras in the early 1980s. Fidel Martinez Rodriguez founded and named the organization after a 19th-century Honduran peasant leader, Serapio "Cinchonero" Romero, who was executed in 1865 for refusing to pay church taxes. After Rodriguez's death in June 1981, leadership fell into unknown hands.

The most famous terrorist act by this group was the seizure of the Chamber of Commerce building in San Pedro del Sula in September 1982. The 12 members who participated in this operation received asylum in Cuba later that month. This group was active in 1983 and 1984, but less has been heard from them since the arrest of most of its leaders in 1984.

Communist Combatant Cells (Cellules Communistes Combattantes) (CCC) (Belgium)

The founder of this group, Pierre Carette, was influenced by the leaders of Action Directe. It emerged from obscurity in October 1984 with an attack on Litton Data Systems in Belgium. For a long time police thought that this organization was part of Action Directe, but the capture of some documents in 1985 proved its distinct identity.

While the CCC membership may never have been larger than 10, it carried out more than 20 deadly bombings in Belgium during 1984–1985. The CCC was extremely active and efficient in its actions, primarily targeting NATO installations in a bombing campaign. The arrest of Carette and other leaders in December 1985 caused the survivors to go underground, and most of its members have drifted away while he remains in prison.

Contras (Nicaragua)

This right-wing terrorist organization is a combination of the Nicaraguan Armed Revolutionary Forces (FARN), the Nicaraguan Democratic Force (FDN), and other anti-Sandinista groups. These groups united in the early 1980s to fight the Sandinista government with the financial help of the U.S. government.

Leaders of the largest group, the FDN, were Adolfo Calero and Engrique Bermudez. Two other prominent leaders were Eden Pastora and Alfonso Robelo, but because of the decentralized nature of military operations, leadership always remained at the local level. Contra forces numbered between 12,000 and 15,000 until they were disbanded in the aftermath of the electoral defeat of the Sandinistas in 1989. Many of the Contras had been supporters of the pre-Sandinista right-wing government of Somoza, and some of them are still unhappy with the new moderate Chamoro government.

Coordination of United Revolutionary Organizations (CORU) (United States)

Most of the anti-Castro Cuban organizations came together during the mid-1970s to form this group. Orlando Bosch was the recognized leader until he was arrested in October 1976 and imprisoned in Venezuela for the bombing of a Cuban airliner. His release a few years later did little to revitalize this group. While this organization operated out of Miami, most of its terrorist activities were carried on outside of the United States, including several assassinations and bombings in 1976 and 1977. It has since disappeared.

Croatian Revolutionary Brotherhood (Hrvatsko Revolucionarno Bratstvo) (HRB) (Yugoslavia)

This organization was part of a Croatian separatist effort that grew out of the Croatian Liberation Movement, which had a history of fascist collaboration. The HRB, also called the Ustashi, espoused the re-establishment of a Croatian state from the Yugoslavian state. It is nationalistic with fascist tendencies, and members are furiously anti-Serbian. Some of its members cooperated with the German army in operations against Serbs during World War II. Only a small cadre has been involved with terrorism, possibly as few as 30, but the Croatian community has considerable sympathy for the aims of HRB. Terrorists acts have been committed by members of this group against Yugoslav officials in Europe and the United States. The creation of an independent Croatia in 1991 ended most of the terrorist activities of this group. Even the civil war with Serbia during the winter of 1991 and 1992 failed to revitalize it.

Cuban National Liberation Front (FLNC) (United States)

FLNC has conducted anti-Castro activities in the United States and in Cuba. Its avowed goal is the overthrow of Fidel Castro, but beyond this it has uncertain plans for Cuba. José de la Torrient was the head of this Miami-based group and the coordinator of targets. FLNC attacked Cuban targets both in Cuba and in the United States in the 1970s. This group was less active during the 1980s, but many members are still active in anti-Castro politics.

Death Squad (Esquadrao da Morte) (Brazil)

The Death Squad was a Brazilian right-wing terrorist group that operated in the 1970s. It was organized sometime in the late 1960s by Sergio Parahhos Fleury, and it aimed to eliminate all persons with anti-government tendencies.

The majority of the Death Squad's membership consisted of off-duty policemen disgusted with Brazil's inefficient judicial system. Most of their victims were terrorists or left-wing sympathizers, but petty criminals were also arrested, tortured, and executed along with the terrorists. It has been estimated that of the 21,000 people arrested by the Death Squad during the 1970s, about 4,000 were executed. It was this group that organized the ambush that killed Action for National Liberation terrorist Carlos Marighella in 1969.

Democratic Front for the Liberation of Palestine (DFLP) (Palestine)
The DFLP broke away from the PFLP in 1969 over a dispute about tactics. Although this group has a distinct Marxist-Leninist political orientation, it has always subordinated terrorist activities to political maneuvering.

The leader of the DFLP is a Greek Orthodox Christian, Nayef Hawatmeh. Membership is only about 1,000, and in the past it received financial and moral support from the former Soviet Union and China. While some of its members have engaged in sporadic terrorist activity, such as an attack on an Israeli school bus in 1974, this type of terrorism has been discouraged by DFLP leadership. Although an active member of the PLO, much of its political clout was ended after the defeat of the PLO in Lebanon during the early 1980s.

EOKA (Ethniki Organosis Kyprion Agoniston) (National Organization of Cypriot Fighters) (Cyprus)
This Greek Cypriot terrorist organization carried out a violent campaign in Cyprus for nearly five years during the late 1950s aimed at uniting Cyprus with Greece. George Grivas, the military commander, and Archbishop Makarios, the head of the political wing, combined to drive the British out of Cyprus.

The EOKA devised a strategy of sabotage, attacks on British forces, and civil disobedience. Slightly more than a thousand EOKA terrorists carried out assassinations, bombings, and political agitation. Despite this violence, internal dissension, active Turkish minority opposition, and British resolve prevented EOKA's success. The British sent 30,000 troops to Cyprus in an effort to end terrorism, but these troops were never able to capture the leaders of EOKA.

Cyprus was granted independence, but without union with Greece. Soon afterward, Grivas and Makarios became rivals, and Grivas reconstituted his terrorist group in 1971 as EOKA-B. This group had 800 activists and another 2,000 auxiliaries. EOKA-B was outlawed in 1974, but it was the death of Grivas that weakened the movement. He was replaced by his next-in-command, Nikos Glorgiades (Sampson). With the help of the Greek government, Glorgiades overthrew the Makarios regime. This new government, however, was soon weakened by the Turkish invasion of Cyprus and the overthrow of Glorgiades's sponsors in Greece. Glorgiades was arrest in March 1976 for his role in the coup of 1974.

Eritrean Liberation Front (ELF) (Ethiopia)
This organization has been active in terrorist activities directed against the Ethiopian government and its military forces since the mid-1960s. Formed by a group of exiles (Ibrahim Sultan, Osman Saleh Sabbeh, and Welde-Ab Welde-Miriam) in Cairo in 1958, the ELF goal is a separate state for the Eritrean provinces of Ethiopia. Idris Mohammed Adem, the head of ELF's General Command, and Osman Saleh Sabbeh, the head of the armed units, have been the principal leaders.

While this group has engaged in bombings, aircraft hijacking, and attacks on Ethiopian government property, it specialized in kidnappings, especially during the late 1960s and 1970s. Ideological conflict in 1975 caused a schism in the ELF with the radical wing forming the Popular Liberation Force (PLF). A political truce was formed shortly afterward, and both groups directed their energies toward a non-Marxist government.

In 1977, the ELF had nearly 22,000 guerrillas in the field. Another split took place in 1981, and fierce in-fighting caused the ELF to lose many of its supporters to the Eritrean People's Liberation Front (EPLF). During the mid-1980s, this group transformed itself into part of a military alliance to overthrow the leftist Ethiopian government, an effort that was successful in 1991.

Euskadi Ta Askatasuna (ETA) (Spain)
The ETA, or Basque Nation and Freedom, is a terrorist group formed in 1959 to fight for Basque independence from Spain. It grew out of the opposition Basque Nationalist Party (PNV). While this new organization started out with a vague Marxist-Leninist orientation, it was reoriented by new leadership to a national liberation movement in the late 1960s. The ETA assassination of the Spanish Prime Minister, Admiral Carrero Blanco, in 1973 changed the course of political life in Spain.

The ETA has had a variety of leaders, but Francisco Javier Echevarrieta Ortiz, until his death in June 1968, Eustakio Mendizabal Benito, until his death in April 1973, and Moreno Berareche have been the most prominent. Estimates of its active membership range from 50 to 200, but it has thousands of sympathizers. Members operate in three-person cells for security reasons. Many members have received training in PLO camps, and the group keeps in contact with other European terrorist groups.

The ETA has been subject to internal division on terrorist strategy, and in the late 1970s it split into two competing wings. While ETA-PM began acting like a political party, ETA-M became active in terrorism. Leaders of ETA-M have been José Mique Benaran Ordenana, Maria Dolores Gonzalez Catatain, and Anton Echeviesti. Both ETA groups became less active in the 1980s because of efforts by the Spanish government to grant more political autonomy to the Basque region.

Al-Fatah (Palestine National Liberation Movement) (Palestine)
Al-Fatah is the oldest of the Palestinian terrorist groups. It was formally founded in 1962, but it was active in earlier forms, beginning in the mid-1950s. Al-Fatah was initially formed to fight against Israel, and its strategy was based upon the successful terrorism of the Algerian FLN.

Al-Fatah's military wing, al-Asifah, commenced operations against Israel in 1965. In 1968 this group joined the PLO, and in the next year the leader of al-Fatah, Yasser Arafat, was elected chairman of the PLO Executive Committee. After a series of terrorist acts in the 1970s, this organization stressed a political rather than military solution to the Palestinian question.

Al-Fatah has an active membership of about 7,000. Much of its financial support has come from Saudi Arabia, Kuwait, and other moderate Persian Gulf States. The PLO's support of Iraq during the Persian Gulf War threatens the longterm financial support received by al-Fatah from these countries. The assassinations of Abu Iyad, the chief of PLO intelligence and a key figure in al-Fatah, and Hayil Abd al-Hamid, al-Fatah's security chief, in January 1992 has weakened al-Fatah's leadership.

Federation of European National Action (Federation d'Action Nationale Européene) (FANE)/European National Fascists (Faisceaux Nationales Europeenes) (FNE) (France)
FANE/FNE is a French right-wing terrorist organization founded in 1966. Marc Fredrikson, a former bank clerk, has been one of the group's leaders. Its members publicize their views in the racist journal *Notre Europe*. In an investigation of its 200 active members in 1980, almost one-fifth of its members were found to be police officers.

FANE was banned in 1980 because of its terrorism, and FNE was formed shortly afterward to take its place. They have participated in bombings and in vandalism, particularly directed toward Jewish targets. Though the assassination of Jewish activist Pierre Goldman in 1977 was carried out by another group, l'Honneur de la Police, it appears to have close ties to FANE/FNE.

First of October Anti-Fascist Resistance Group (Grupo de Resistencia Antifascista Primo de Octubre) (GRAPO) (Spain)
GRAPO is a radical splinter group of the Spanish Communist Party. It was formed in the mid-1970s to destabilize the Spanish government. Its leaders have been Abelardo Collazo, before his arrest in Madrid in 1976, Fernando Hierro, until his arrest in Madrid in 1977, Enriqué Cerdan Calixto, who was killed by police in Madrid in 1981, and José Maria Sanchez Casas. An open battle between GRAPO and the Spanish police developed with significant casualties on both sides. GRAPO has always been a small group, especially since the Spanish police have managed to infiltrate their ranks.

Frente Farabundo Marti De Liberacion Nacional (FMLN)
(El Salvador)
The FMLN serves as the umbrella organization for the groups fighting to overthrow the El Salvadoran government. While several of the groups espouse Marxist-Leninist ideals, the membership has a variety of political agendas.

Membership in the FMLN is probably in the thousands with widespread support among rural people. Its leadership coordinates the military and terrorist campaign against the government. Evidence is available that some support in equipment and training has come from Cuba, Nicaragua, and the former Soviet bloc, but the extent of this support remains uncertain.

Members of FMLN have attacked American personnel and targets on occasion, but the usual operations are against the El Salvadoran government and military. Peace negotiations in late 1991 and early 1992 ended with the FMLN disbanding in exchange for the government's reduction in military forces.

Front for the Liberation of Brittany (FLB)/Breton Republican Army (ARB) (France)
These two groups joined to form a single terrorist organization whose purpose is to separate Brittany from the French state. This organization is an outgrowth of the peaceful separatist Movement for the Organization of Brittany (MOB). The FLB is the political wing and the ARB is the terrorist wing. Membership of both groups numbers between 150 and 200. Some evidence exists that members of this group received training by Irish revolutionaries in 1972. A bombing campaign during the late 1960s ended when 60 members were arrested in 1969. After receiving amnesty in 1971, several members

renewed their efforts to achieve independence through terrorism. Although both wings were outlawed in 1974, this organization continued a bombing campaign against the property of the French state in the late 1970s. Its most publicized bombing was at the Palace of Versailles on June 26, 1978. The arrest of most of FLB-ARB leaders ended this group's effectiveness by 1980. Special efforts by the French government to improve economic conditions in Brittany have helped ease tensions and removed much of the threat of terrorism.

Front for the National Liberation of Corsica (Front de la Liberation Nationale de la Corse) (FLNC) (France)

This organization was formed in 1976 out of several Corsican separatist groups to persuade the French government to grant Corsica independence. Most of its terrorist attacks have been in Corsica or southern France, but an occasional bombing has taken place in Paris. Its members specialize in bombings of French administrative buildings and military installations. FLNC was declared illegal in 1983, but this has not reduced its terrorist activities. While activists only number about 200, they have received considerable support from the Corsican people.

Grey Wolves (Turkey)

This right-wing Turkish nationalist group was founded by Colonel Alparslan Turkes during the early 1970s to fight against communism and democratic institutions. Estimates place the strength of the Grey Wolves at several thousand fighters. It conducted a terrorist campaign against moderate Turkish politicians as well as left-wing groups, specializing in the assassination of political opponents.

The Grey Wolves were in the middle of a civil war with left-wing terrorist groups when the military coup of 1980 ended open warfare. Many members of the Grey Wolves, including Colonel Turkes, were tried for their crimes during the early 1980s. Some evidence is available that his group used the drug trade to finance its terrorist activities.

Hezbollah (Party of God) (Lebanon)

This Lebanese Shi'ite terrorist group was founded in Beirut, Lebanon, by Sheikh Muhammed Hassan Fadlallah in 1982 out of parts of the Islamic Amal and the Islamic al-Dawa. Tactical control was maintained by Sheik Abbas Mussawi until his death in March 1992.

Hezbollah has been estimated as having only 700 members, but its militia strength may be as high as 4,000. Most of its recruits are young

Shi'ites from the poorest segments of Lebanese society who are sometimes trained for suicide missions. It receives direct moral and financial support from Iran. Specializing in kidnappings and hostage-taking, Hezbollah directs most of its activities toward Israeli, American, and European targets. The death of Iran's Khomeini seems to have moderated the terrorist activities of this group, as made evident by the release of American and European hostages in late 1991.

Hoffman Military-Sports Group (West Germany)
The Hoffman Military-Sports Group is a right-wing terrorist organization specializing in anti-Jewish acts. It was founded by Karl Heinz Hoffman in the late 1970s. Active membership is probably under a hundred, but sympathizers number in the thousands. This group has had a close working relationship with the PLO, and some evidence exists that members have received PLO training. Members specialize in bombings, assassinations, and destruction of Jewish property. Its most famous terrorist act was the bombing of the 1980 Munich Fest. The West German government banned this group in 1980, and Hoffman was arrested in 1981 and charged with murder. Many ex-members have joined other right-wing political groups in the resurgence of neo-Nazi activity in reunited Germany.

Independent Republic of the South Moluccas (The Netherlands)
This terrorist movement grew out of discontent among South Moluccan refugees in The Netherlands during the 1970s. These refugees had come to The Netherlands after Indonesia won its independence in 1949. Young members of the community launched a terrorist campaign to gain South Moluccan independence from Indonesia. A series of bombings and several train hijackings in the mid- and late-1970s were the extent of their terrorist activities. Activists numbered about 250, but they had considerable support among the 40,000 members of the South Moluccan community. Most of the activists are serving prison terms in Dutch jails.

Irgun Zvai Leumi-be-Israel (National Military Organization of Israel) (Israel)
This organization was the largest Jewish terrorist group active in the years before the partition of Palestine. It started out as the military army of the Revisionist Party of Vladimir Jabotinsky, but it soon became more significant than its party. David Raziel was the founder of the Irgun, but he was killed in Iraq in 1943, and future Israeli Prime Minister Menachem Begin took his place. The Irgun carried out a

violent terrorist campaign against the British military government of Palestine between 1942 and 1947. Many of the present political leaders of Israel were once Irgun members. Its most publicized act was the bombing of the King David Hotel in Jerusalem, which killed at least 89 people. Members of this group became hostile to the other prominent Jewish terrorist group, the Stern Gang. Irgun was incorporated into the Israeli army during the war in 1948 with many of its leaders becoming prominent in right-wing Israeli political parties.

Irish National Liberation Army (INLA) (Northern Ireland)
The Irish National Liberation Army (INLA) is the newest of the Irish terrorist groups fighting to unify Ireland. This Marxist group split away from the IRA in 1975, and soon afterward, INLA leader Sean Costello was shot in Dublin by the IRA.

INLA headquarters are in Dublin, where it recruits terrorists for attacks in Northern Ireland. INLA conducts terrorist operations against the same type of targets as the IRA-Provisional Wing (Provos), so it is difficult to distinguish between their operations. This group was especially active in kidnappings, assassinations, and bombings during the 1980s. Other Irish terrorist groups consider members of INLA as "the wild men" in the struggle for Northern Ireland.

Irish Republican Army (IRA) (Republic of Ireland)
The IRA is one of the oldest political-terrorist organizations still in operation. Its roots go back to the struggle for an independent Ireland in the nineteenth century, and the Irish Republican Brotherhood. The IRA started out as the paramilitary wing of the Sinn Fein (Ourselves Alone) Party, and it fought a vicious war against the British in Ireland between 1918 and 1921. After the formation of the Irish Free State, the IRA lost a two-year war against the new republic and most of its activities were moved underground.

Despite repudiation of its program by the Irish Republic, the IRA still has substantial moral and financial support among the Catholic Irish in Ireland and Northern Ireland. The goal of this organization is to unify the six northern counties of Ireland with the Republic of Ireland. Members of this organization have been engaged in a long terrorist campaign to drive out British forces from Northern Ireland and to counter the political influence of the Protestant Irish of Ulster. The IRA's pronounced Marxist orientation caused some Irish Catholics to transfer their support to the IRA-Provos, but the reorientation of the Provos toward quasi-Marxism has modified this attraction.

While this organization has not been as violent as the IRA-Provos, its members have engaged in sporadic terrorist activity. A considerable part of the financial support for the IRA comes from its Irish-American supporters. Leaders of the IRA have included Cathal Goulding, Sean Garland, and Liam Macmillan, but most recently Gerry Adams has become its leading figure.

Irish Republican Army Provisional Wing (IRA-Provos) (Northern Ireland)

The IRA-Provos, or Provisional IRA (PIRA), constitutes the IRA's radical, nationalist splinter group. It was formed in 1969 by militant members of the IRA to protest the IRA's more moderate policies. Their goal was to free Northern Ireland by following the same military-political formula used to gain independence for Algeria. The strategy has been to make Ulster ungovernable and to drive the British to withdraw support from the Protestants.

At first the leadership of the IRA-Provos repudiated the Marxist philosophy of the IRA and replaced it with one based on Irish nationalism, but more recent leaders have readopted a vague Marxist orientation. Active members have been estimated at between 300 and 1,000, but supporters probably number in the thousands. In addition to terrorist attacks against British supporters in Northern Ireland, members of this group have engaged in bombings and assassinations in Great Britain, but the group has also branched out into legitimate business undertakings in Belfast. Irish Americans have provided much of the group's financial and moral support. Relations between the IRA-Provos and the IRA are not cordial, though fighting between them is rare. Leading members have been Ruairi O'Bradaigh, Sean MacStiofain (chief of staff from 1969 to 1974), David O'Connell, Seamus Twomey, and Martin McGuinness.

Islamic Amal (al-Mal al-Islami) (Lebanon)

The Islamic Amal is a Lebanese Shi'ite terrorist group that split from the Amal in 1979. Its leader has been Hussein Mussawi, a former schoolteacher. Its active membership numbers about 1,000, mostly located in the Bekaa Valley of Lebanon. After a brief successful struggle against the Amal, this group has undertaken a series of suicide missions resulting in widespread casualties and property loss. It has also cultivated good relations with the Syrians who occupy the Bekaa Valley. The exact relationship between the Islamic Amal and the Islamic Jihad has never been ascertained, but both carry out policies decided by Iranian authorities.

Islamic Jihad (Holy War) (Iran)
This Shi'ite fundamentalist terrorist organization serves as an umbrella body for several terrorist groups. Many of its supporters came out of the Amal movement, but the most active participants have been the Hezbollah and the Islamic Amal.

Islamic Jihad first appeared as a separate entity in 1983 with the October suicide attack on the U.S. marines at Beirut Airport. It gained further notoriety after a series of bombings in 1985. While most of the terrorists live in Lebanon, their group receives its main support from Iran; it may also receive some support from the Syrian government. Most of the terrorist attacks have occurred in Europe and the Middle East, and they are directed against any target that is perceived to be a threat to Iran. Members of this group have been especially active in the hostage-taking of Americans and Europeans remaining in Lebanon.

Japanese Red Army (Sekigun-ha) (JRA) (Japan)
Takaya Shiomi, a former Kyoto University student, founded this organization in 1969 from remnants of dissatisfied Communist student groups. His arrest and imprisonment in 1970 ended his role as leader. It remains a unique organization in that a woman, Fusako Shigenobu, has been its leader for more than twenty years. Membership only numbers about 70, and the active terrorist wing has only about 30 members.

A factional dispute in May 1972 resulted in the death of 14 revisionist members. Most JRA terrorist activities took place in the early 1970s. Among the most bloody was an attack on Lod Airport in 1972. Its leadership always worked closely with the PFLP; it became so dependent on PFLP financial support that some accused it of losing its organizational autonomy. Little was heard from this terrorist group in the late 1970s, and in 1981 Shigenobu renounced the use of terror by the JRA. Several JRA operations have been reported since 1986, indicating that Shinegobu's announcement was premature. The most publicized operation conducted by the JRA was the bombing of a CSO club in Naples, Italy, in April 1988.

Jewish Defense League (JDL) (United States)
Rabbi Meir Kahane founded the JDL in 1968 as a Jewish protective organization, but it soon developed an armed campaign against

anti-Jewish interests. At first the JDL patrolled the streets of Brooklyn to protect people from crime, but anger at the anti-Israeli policies of the former Soviet Union and the Arab states caused its members to turn to violence. The new strategy of this group was to harass Soviet authorities in the United States, but gradually the members turned to terrorism. Paramilitary training camps were set up in California and in the Catskill Mountains of upstate New York during the 1980s to train members.

Terrorist activities, including assassinations, bombings, and vandalism, have been conducted by members of this organization. Primary targets remain Arab officials. The assassination of Kahane in November 1990 removed the JDL's leader but not its political influence in New York City and Israel. Unhappiness with the acquittal of the alleged assassin by a New York jury in early 1992 may revitalize the activities of the JDL in the United States.

Justice Commandos of the Armenian Genocide (JCAG)
(Europe/United States)
This organization is a right-wing Armenian nationalist terrorist group devoted to revenge attacks against Turkey for past crimes against Armenians. JCAG was founded in 1975 as a right-wing counterpart to the left-wing ASALA, but it has ties to Dashnaq, a longstanding Armenian political party with a history of moderation. While the goals and tactics of JCAG and ASALA are identical, ideological differences make it impossible for them to work together. Members of JCAG have conducted numerous attacks on Turkish diplomats and property. Activity patterns indicate that only a small cadre exists to carry out its terrorist campaign. Financial support comes from conservative elements in the Armenian communities of Europe and the United States.

Lebanese Armed Revolutionary Faction (Factions Armées Revolutionnaires Libanaises) (FARL)(Lebanon)
FARL is a Lebanese Christian terrorist group founded by George Ibrahim Abdullah. Despite its Christian background, the leadership of this group espouses a Marxist-Leninist ideology. Most of its membership is recruited from the two small northern Lebanon villages of Qubayat and Andaqat. It receives financial support from Syria. Many of its activities are directed toward Israeli and Jewish targets. Most of its violent acts have been bombings in Paris, and its members have often cooperated with the French left-wing terrorist group Action Directe. Abdullah was captured by French police in 1984, and FARL

conducted a violent bombing campaign in France during most of 1986 to free him.

M-19 (Movimiento 19 Abril) (Colombia)

This terrorist group was active in the 1980s. Founded in 1974 by Carlos Toledo Plata and Jamie Bateman Cayon to promote revolution in Colombia, its name comes from a disputed presidential election in 1970. Toledo was captured by Colombian anti-terrorist forces in 1981, and Bateman assumed sole leadership. Bateman was formerly a member of the FARC, but despite close ties between Bateman and the leadership of FARC, disagreements over strategy and tactics kept the two groups apart. After Bateman's death in a plane crash in April 1983, Carlos Toledo Plata succeeded him. Plata was assassinated in August 1984 by a paramilitary death squad. M-19's next leader, Ivan Marino Ospina, was killed in August 1985 by the Colombian army.

The original strategy of this group was to destabilize the Colombian state by a selective strategy of robberies, kidnappings for ransom, and assassinations. The current leader of M-19 appears to be Carlos Pizarro and its membership includes about 1,000 activists. Its most publicized terrorist act was the seizure of the Palace of Justice in Bogotá in November 1985, which caused the loss of 50 operatives, including one of the leaders, Luis Otero. Financial support has come from both the former Soviet Union and Cuba. A close connection was formed in the mid-1980s by this group and Colombian drug rings. Some evidence is available that this group is engaged in large-scale drug running to raise funds for its cause. M-19 and the Colombian government signed an agreement on November 2, 1989 which stated that M-19 would disband as a guerrilla force and its members would become integrated into society. It remains unclear how long this agreement will remain in place.

Montoneros (Argentina)

The Montoneros terrorist organization started out as an ultra-Catholic wing of the Peron Party, but it became more left-wing as its terrorist campaign progressed. By 1973, it had become the unsanctioned guerrilla wing of the Peronist Party. Montoneros activities were directed toward a war of liberation rather than traditional party politics. Mario Firmenich was the operational leader of the Montoneros after his release from prison in 1973, but most of the leadership disappeared in the crackdown of the late 1970s. Members engaged in assassinations, bombings, and kidnappings. In 1973, it had an active membership of well over a thousand, and supporters in the hundreds of thousands. The right-wing terrorist campaign after 1976 diminished its strength and it is now almost extinct. Its leaders cooperated closely with the People's Revolutionary Army (ERP) in the 1970s, and this alliance still operates.

National Liberation Front (Front de Liberation Nationale) (FLN) (Algeria)

This organization fought a war of national liberation for Algeria to escape from French colonial rule. It was organized in 1954 out of various Algerian nationalist groups. A former bakery worker, Yacef Saadi, was the operational leader of the FLN while Ahmed Ben Bella was the political leader. This organization used a pragmatic and distinctly Algerian nationalist orientation. It was not until 1962 that it adopted socialist principles. The military side of the FLN was the Army of National Liberation (ALN). Using a combination of low-intensity warfare techniques and terrorism, this organization stalemated French forces and won independence for Algeria in 1962. The success of the FLN set an example for every nationalist terrorist group since the 1960s.

National Vanguard (Avanguardia Nazionale) (AN) (Italy)

This right-wing extremist organization was founded in 1960 as a splinter group of the New Order. Stefano Delle Chiaie organized this group as the terrorist wing of the neo-fascist movement. At its peak, the National Vanguard could boast of about 500 activists who often clashed with left-wing students and attacked adherents of the Italian Communist Party. Delle Chiaie formally dissolved this group in 1965, but it reappeared in 1970 in much the same form. It re-allied with the New Order in 1975 to conduct joint operations against its left-wing opposition. Evidence has appeared that this group received legal protection from elements in the Italian intelligence service, the Servizio Informazione Difensa (SID), until 1975. Authorities banned the National Vanguard in 1976, and Delle Chiaie escaped to South America. Many members joined the Armed Revolutionary Nuclei (NAR) after 1979.

New Order-Black Order (Ordine Nuovo-Ordine Nero) (Italy)

Most of this right-wing terrorist group's leaders were former members of the neofascist Italian Social Movement (MSI), but they left because of the proposed alliance of the MSI with conservative political parties in 1956. The leaders, Guisippe Rauti, Franco Freda, Clemente Graziani, Paolo Signorelli, and Stefano Delle Chiaie, were able to recruit thousands of adherents to this group. It was not until the mid-1960s that this group and their allies, the National Vanguard, resorted to terrorism.

In 1970, the New Order consisted of about 1,500 active members, but their numbers dropped during the late 1970s. Street riots and bombings led Italian authorities to prosecute the New Order leaders in 1974. Both the New Order and the National Vanguard were outlawed, and most of their leaders fled Italy. Many members of the New Order migrated to a new group, the Black Order. This new group's most violent act was a train bombing in August 1974 that killed or injured 60 people. Some evidence exists that both the New Order and the Black Order continued former ties with MSI. It has also been revealed that both groups enjoyed support from police and security officers.

New People's Army (NPA) (Philippines)

The NPA is the guerrilla arm of the Communist Party of the Philippines. This Marxist-Leninist organization was founded in 1969 with the goal of overthrowing the Philippine government of Ferdinand Marcos. Although most of its past activities were restricted to the countryside, the group has expanded its network into the cities. Estimates of activists range from 18,000 to 20,000, with widespread public support. This organization has specialized in the execution of government officials and those seen as enemies of the class struggle. Assassination teams known as the Sparrow Squads restricted their targets to Philippine citizens until 1987, after the ceasefire following the overthrow of Marcos ended. Their primary targets then became U.S. servicemen, especially with the controversy over the renewal of the military bases.

Omega 7 (United States)

Omega 7 is the most violent right-wing Cuban exile terrorist group in existence. This group appeared suddenly in 1975, and many of its members had contacts in the Cuban Nationalist Movement, as well as in an earlier terrorist organization, Alpha 66. Two of its leaders were Eduardo Arocena and Orlando Bosch, both of whom served long prison terms for terrorist activities.

Omega 7's avowed goal is to overthrow the Castro government. Only about 100 activists engage in terrorism, but U.S. authorities have traced at least 30 terrorist incidents to the group during the late 1970s. Its members have also engaged in selective assassinations of Cuban diplomats. While this group has little hope of overthrowing the Castro regime, it effectively discouraged American citizens from engaging in business or personal relationships with the Cuban government.

Organization of the Secret Army (Organization de l'Armée Secréte (OAS) (France)
This terrorist group was organized to keep the French government from granting independence to Algeria. A group of French officers founded this organization, but its nominal leader was General Salan. Robert Degueldre was the operational commander, and his leadership of the "Delta" squads made the OAS a force to be feared. It conducted assassinations and bombings against French supporters of Algerian independence and against Algerians. After the granting of independence to Algeria, the OAS launched several assassination attempts against the President of France, Charles de Gaulle. Many OAS members were either former or active-duty soldiers during its terrorist campaign. Only after the arrest and imprisonment of most of its leadership did the OAS stop its terrorist campaign. Degueldre was considered by the French army to be the most dangerous member of the OAS, and he was executed by firing squad in July 1962.

Palestine Liberation Front (PLF) (Palestine)
One of the many splinter groups that broke away from the PFLP-GC is the PLF. The original split was in the mid-1970s, but ideological friction in the new group caused it to break up again into pro-PLO, pro-Syrian, and pro-Libyan factions. Muhammad Abbas (also called Abu Abbas) became head of the dominant pro-PLO faction. He also became a member of the PLO Executive Committee in 1984. The PLF has only about 50 active members, but they have conducted a variety of terrorist operations; its most famous was the seizure of the cruise ship *Achille Lauro* in October 1985. Most sources indicate that this group has operated out of Iraq for the last several years.

Palestine Liberation Organization (PLO) (Palestine)
The Palestine Liberation Organization (PLO) commands the campaign of the Palestinians against Israel, pressing for the formation of a Palestinian state. It shelters five terrorist groups, al-Fatah, al-Sa'iga, PFLP, PFLP-GC, and the Popular Democratic Front for the Liberation of Palestine (PDFLP), and as many as 15 social and educational associations. An Arab summit conference in January 1964 proposed— and a Palestinian Congress in April 1964 established—the PLO.

The first leader of the PLO was Ahmed Shuqairy, a Palestinian diplomat, until his leadership was discredited in the aftermath of the

1967 Arab-Israeli War. Yasser Arafat's al-Fatah group became the dominant faction in 1969. The change in orientation from terrorism to politics in 1974 led to a schism, with dissenters forming the Rejectionist Front. While ideological debates have hindered the work of the PLO, it has received official recognition by most Arabs and Palestinians as the sole and legitimate voice of the Palestinian people. Though the eviction of the PLO from Beirut in 1982 weakened it, its influence remained. No settlement of the Palestinian question can take place without the PLO playing a role. Yasser Arafat has been able to withstand numerous attacks against his leadership, but he remains so important to the organization, it is unclear what may happen should he die, be killed, or leave the PLO.

People's Liberation Organization of Tamil Eelam (PLOTE) (Sri Lanka)
This Marxist-Leninist organization has led an active terrorist campaign since 1977 to create a separate Tamil state in northern Sri Lanka. Dr. Anton Balasingham is the political theorist and Rajan Nithian is the head of PLOTE. The Liberation Tigers of Tamil Eelam (LTTE) is the military wing of this organization headed by V. Prabhakaran. The hard-core terrorist membership of PLOTE and other allied groups has been estimated at about 600, but sympathizers number in the thousands. This group has fought a mini-civil war in Sri Lanka, using assassinations, bombings, and other methods of low-intensity warfare. Most of its moral and financial support has come from the Tamil population in southern India. Some evidence suggests that the assassination of former Indian Prime Minister Rajiv Gandhi was carried out by members of this group.

People's Revolutionary Army (Ejercito Revolucionario des Pueblo) **(ERP)** (Argentina)
This Argentinian urban terrorist and rural guerrilla organization threatened to overthrow the Argentinian state for a period in the middle 1970s. It was founded in 1970 by Mario Roberto Santucho Juarez as the armed wing of the Trotskyite Workers' Revolutionary Party (PRT). The goal of this organization was to overthrow the capitalist system in Argentina and then other governments in the rest of South America. By 1974, it is estimated that the ERP had more than 2,000 activists and some 12,000 dependable supporters. Members of ERP conducted kidnappings, bank robberies, and assassinations, becoming so powerful as a military force that units of the ERP engaged Argentine military troops in combat in 1975. The subsequent loss of

its two major leaders, Roberto Santucho and José Urteaga, during a gun battle in Buenos Aires in July 1976 weakened the leadership of the movement. Nevertheless, the ERP became so successful in mobilizing supporters for social revolution that a right-wing counterterrorist organization, the Argentine Anti-Communist Alliance (AAA), was formed to fight against it. A reign of terror ensued in the late 1970s that almost wiped out the ERP. While the ERP still exists today in Argentina, it remains a much weakened organization.

Popular Democratic Front for the Liberation of Palestine (PDFLP) (Palestine)
Another dissident offshoot from the PFLP, this group conducts terrorist operations against Israeli targets. Nayef Hawatmeh formed this organization out of PFLP members, and he serves as its principal spokesperson. The PDFLP is ideologically well to the left of al-Fatah, but it has been an active participant in PLO activities. This group is reputed to have had close contacts with both the former Soviet Union and Syria. It has always been a small group, with an estimated strength of only 500 devotees, and the defeat of the PLO in Lebanon has weakened it.

Popular Front for the Liberation of Palestine (PFLP) (Palestine)
The PFLP is one of the oldest Palestinian terrorist groups. It was founded, in December 1967, by Dr. George Habash, a physician trained at the American University in Beirut. It combined three smaller terrorist groups: the Youth of Vengeance, the Return Heroes, and the Palestinian Liberation Front. The tactical leader of the PFLP was Dr. Wadi Haddad until his death in 1978. Active membership is between 500 and 800, but it can always count on a larger number of sympathizers. While it is part of the PLO, this group often conducts independent operations. The leadership shares a Marxist-Leninist orientation, and they have been opposed to a political settlement with Israel. This group, in 1968, was the first of the Palestinian terrorist groups to internationalize the Israeli-Palestinian conflict by moving terrorist acts outside of the Middle East. Several Arab states support this group (mostly Syria and Libya), but it is currently based in South Yemen. The PFLP was especially active in aircraft hijackings during the late 1960s and 1970s.

Popular Front for the Liberation of Palestine—General Command (PFLP-GC) (Palestine)
This PFLP splinter group was founded in 1968 by Ahmad Jebril, a former Syrian army captain, after he and others became dissatisfied

with Habash's leadership. His complaint was that the PFLP spent too much time on politics and not enough time fighting. Estimates place the membership of this group from as high as 500 to as low as 250 active adherents. Financial and moral support for terrorist activities comes mostly from Syria, but occasionally from Libya. Its headquarters and base of operations was in Beirut, but has been moved to Damascus, Syria. Members of this organization have specialized in suicide operations, predominantly against Israel. Jebril has sometimes opposed Arafat's policies in the PLO, but his group remains a member of the larger organization.

Posse Comitatus (United States)

Henry Lamont Beach founded this group in 1968 to oppose federal taxation and federal control. Members recognize the county sheriff as the highest officer of the law under their interpretation of the U.S. Constitution. Several members have been involved in shootings and kidnappings. Most members are armed vigilantes and survivalists, and they expect the overthrow of the United States by left-wing subversives.

Quebec Liberation Front (Front Liberation du Quebec) (FLQ) (Canada)

Formed in 1963 as a loose group of youths from French-speaking Quebec seeking to promote the independence of Quebec from the rest of Canada, this group had a short but effective career in terrorism. The Canadian authorities estimated the FLQ strength in 1970 to be 130 terrorists and about 2,000 active sympathizers, with much of its strength from lower-middle-class members. This group started out with small-scale robberies and bombings, but graduated to kidnapping and murder. While no discernible central leadership ever emerged from the FLQ, Pierre Vallierè and Charles Gagnon provided the left-wing philosophy for the group. Two factions of this group were involved in separate kidnappings in the early 1970s that resulted in the death of the Canadian Minister of Labor, Pierre Laporte. The Trudeau government invoked the War Measures Act to gain the police authority to track down the terrorists.

Rebel Armed Forces (FAR) (Guatemala)

Among the more active terrorist groups in Central America during the late 1960s and early 1970s was FAR. Yon Sosa, a young army officer, and Turcios Lima led the group until Lima's death in a car accident in 1966. Cesar Montes replaced him as leader. This group's goal was to start a social revolution in Guatemala. Its leaders claimed that the FAR had 20,000 active members, but a more realistic number was several hundred activists. It did have a sympathetic audience among the people of Guatemala. This group specialized in assassination and kidnappings of important figures, notably U.S. officials. The most famous terrorist act by FAR was the kidnapping and murder of the West German Ambassador to Guatemala, Count Karl von Spreti, in March–April 1970. Police activity was able to control this terrorist organization during the late 1970s, with the help of U.S.-trained special forces.

Red Army Faction (RAF) (Germany)
This Marxist-Leninist terrorist group (also known as the Baader-Meinhof Gang) has operated mostly in West Germany, but since reunification, its activities have spread across Germany. Andreas Baader, Ulrike Meinhof, Gudrun Ensslin, and Horst Mahler founded the RAF in 1968 out of the radical wing of the German Socialist Student Alliance (SDS). They attracted a number of anarchist students, and a terrorist campaign was initiated, employing bank robberies and ransom kidnappings. It has an active membership as high as 60, with perhaps 2,000 sympathizers. Hard-core members and sympathizers come from bourgeois and professional families.

The RAF specialize in NATO, West German, and U.S. targets, and they have engaged in bombings, assassinations, kidnappings, and sabotage. Their most famous terrorist act was the kidnapping and murder of the West German industrialist, Hans-Martin Schleyer. The leaders had strong contacts with the Palestinian and Italian Red Brigade terrorist groups. Most of the RAF's leadership was arrested in West German police dragnets during the first three weeks of June 1972. Several of the most important leaders have been imprisoned or have committed suicide, as was the case with Baader, Ensslin, Meinhof, and Jan-Carl Raspe during 1976–1977. Several isolated attacks were made by the RAF in the early 1980s against NATO targets, but West German police pressure resulted in a decrease in RAF activity. New leaders of the RAF were Inge Viett and Christian Klar, but Klar has been imprisoned since his arrest in 1982. A terrorist act conducted by elements of the RAF took place as recently as the summer of 1992. German reunification took away East Germany as a place of sanctuary, but it has not ended the determination of the RAF to use terrorism to promote revolution in Germany.

Red Brigade (Brigate Rosse) (BR) (Italy)

During the 1960s and 1970s, the Italian Red Brigade was the most active and feared terrorist group in Europe. While most of its leaders came out of student and labor unrest in Italy in the late 1960s, it was the anti-Vietnam War agitation that produced the Red Brigade. Its original leaders were a combination of the members of the sociology department at the University of Trent (Renato Curcio, Margherita Cagol, and Giorgio Semeria), former members of Communist youth organizations (Alberto Franceschini, Prospero Galinare) and politicians from other left-wing organizations (Mario Moretti, Piertor Bertolozzi, and Corrado Alunni). The Red Brigade was formed in Milan and members agitated openly for nearly two years before going underground in 1971.

Many of this group's leaders and followers were admirers of the Tupamaros, and so the Red Brigade adopted the Tupamaros organizational structure, instituting terrorist "columns" instead of communist cells. These columns were composed of a large number of terrorists organized around a common mission. Each column had its own leadership and contact between columns was kept at a minimum. At its peak, the Red Brigade's active members numbered between 100 and 250 in most major Italian cities, with at least an additional 1,000 sympathizers. The members specialized in bombings and kidnappings, but after the arrest of several BR leaders, they conducted a vicious campaign of intimidation against the Italian judicial system. Its most publicized terrorist action remains the kidnapping and murder of the prominent Italian politician, Aldo Moro. This event helped mobilize European counterterrorist activity. Evidence shows that the Red Brigade and the Red Army Faction may have worked together during the late 1970s. Most of the leaders of the Red Brigade are either dead or are currently serving long prison terms in Italian jails.

Revolutionary Cells (RZ) (West Germany)

This group is an offshoot of the Baader-Meinhof Gang. It was organized in 1973 as a single cell, but by the end of 1976 it had cells all over Germany. The only recognized leader of this group was Wilfried Boese, but he was killed during the Entebbe raid in 1976. A hijacking by combined RZ and PFLP members ended with the Israeli Defense Force staging a successful rescue at the Entebbe Airport in Uganda. Besides losing its leader in the Entebbe incident, RZ gained no concessions. Members consider themselves part of an armed urban guerrilla movement. Although this group consists of possibly as few as 25 active members, it has conducted an estimated 200 bombings of buildings and prominent political figures. Despite its terrorist record, this group was excluded from the anti-NATO terrorist alliance of 1984 because it was no longer considered large enough to be a viable force in a terrorist campaign.

Sandinista National Liberation Front (FSLN) (Nicaragua)

Founded in 1958 by Carlos Fonsecal Amador, this organization was named after General Augusto Sandino, a rebel against the U.S. occupation of Nicaragua from 1927 to 1933; its members are called Sandinistas. This group used terrorism as a weapon against the conservative Somoza government until a Sandinista-led revolution overthrew it. The ousted opposition formed a military and terrorist organization known as the Contras to fight the Sandinistas. The Sandinistas were voted out of office in 1990, but they still retain control of the military as well as considerable sympathy in the countryside.

Sendero Luminoso (Shining Path) (Peru)

Among the most violent terrorist-insurgency groups in South America, this organization was formed in 1970 by Abimael Guzmán as an Indian-based rural insurgency movement. Its goal was to destroy existing Peruvian institutions and replace them with an Indian-based social revolutionary regime. Terrorist operations were launched in 1980 in a violent campaign of assassinations and intimidations by bombing. Until 1986, the Shining Path restricted its activities to the countryside where it made life difficult for the Peruvian military forces, but since this date the movement has expanded its operations into urban areas. While no accurate estimate exists on the size of this organization, it has recruited enough members from the intelligentsia and the Indian peasantry to constitute a major threat to the Peruvian state.

Members of the Shining Path have specialized in the assassination of government officials and attacks on diplomatic missions. The number of terrorist operations has been estimated to be as high as 12,000, and their dead victims number about 10,000. Peruvian military authorities have conducted an aggressive counterterrorism effort, and much of the original leadership of the group has been wiped out. Guzmán still controls the operations of this group, operating under the nom de guerre of Comrade Gonzalo. Terrorism has become so pervasive in Peru that democratic institutions have been foregone by the current government, which is operating predominately under martial law.

Sikhs (India)
Sikhism is a sixteenth-century offshoot sect of the Hindu religion in India. The adherents adopted a military culture, and most of them live in the Punjab region. Most Sikhs ended up in India after the partition in 1948, but in the 1980s they developed a strong independence movement. Attacks by the Indian Army on the Golden Temple in Amritsar in 1984 and the death of its leader, Sant Jarnail Singh Bhindranwale, have made the Sikhs more militant. Several Sikh organizations have engaged in terrorism—Dal Khalsa, Babbar Khalsa, and the All-India Sikh Students Federation (ASSF). The military arm of the most violent Sikh group, the ASSF, is the Dashmesh Regiment (Tenth Regiment), which is named after a Sikh guru, Gobind Singh, the tenth and last guru. They have adopted tactics such as airline bombings, political assassinations, riots, and demonstrations. It was the assassination of Prime Minister Indira Gandhi by her Sikh bodyguards that has been the most staggering terrorist act by the Sikhs. Sikh terrorists have been less active in the last few years, but they still have the capability and will to launch terrorist campaigns.

Silent Brotherhood (The Order) (United States)
Robert Jay Mathews founded this group, sometimes called The Order, to fight against what he saw as the control of the United States by Communists, Blacks, Catholics, and Jews. He took many of his ideas and the orientation of his group from the *Turner Diaries,* a book published in 1980 by the National Alliance, another right-wing organization. Mathews's goal was to establish a white homeland in the Pacific Northwest. Membership of the Silent Brotherhood fluctuated from 10 to a high of 15 activists. This group specialized in bank and armored-car robberies, counterfeiting, and assassination. Mathews was killed in a gun battle with federal authorities in Washington state in December 1984. Both Mathews and members of his organization had long been active in other white supremacy groups.

South-West African Peoples Organisation (SWAPO) (Namibia)
This left-wing group has been involved in low-intensity warfare in Namibia against South African forces. It was founded in 1960 and its leader is Sam Nujoma. Several former Soviet bloc countries, Cuba, and the former Soviet Union itself had provided military support for its activities. Its 4,000-strong military forces have been based in Angola. The reduction of tension in this region by the withdrawal of Cuban and Soviet aid has caused this organization to restrict its

terrorist activities. It is now one of the largest political parties in Namibia.

Stern Gang (Lohamei Herut Israel) (Fighters for the Freedom of Israel) (Israel)

The Stern Gang, or the Lehi, was a small breakaway faction of the Irgun that conducted a campaign of terror against Arabs and the British in Palestine between 1942 and 1948. Abraham Stern was the founder and acknowledged leader until his capture by British authorities and his subsequent death in an escape attempt in 1942. Yalin-Mor and Yitzhak Shamir succeeded Stern in leadership roles. Membership never exceeded 300 operatives, but as many as 200 young men and women were always active. Members accepted assassinations and bombings as a way to win a Jewish state in Palestine. Relations between the Stern Gang and the Irgun became bitter after Stern's death. Two of the more famous terrorist incidents carried out by the Stern Gang were the assassinations of Lord Moyne in Egypt and of Count Bernadotte in Palestine. While members of the Irgun were incorporated into the Israeli army in 1948, few members of the Stern Gang were invited to join the military forces because Israeli leaders considered Stern members too radical and too difficult to control. Despite this reluctance to admit them into the Israeli power structure, members of the Stern Gang have been active participants in Israeli politics.

Symbionese Liberation Army (SLA) (U.S.A)

The SLA had a brief terrorist career in the early 1970s. Its name comes from an imaginary terrorist group, the Cobras, in Sam Breenlee's book *Who Sat by the Door* (1959). It originated as a group promoting prison reform, but the desire for some type of social revolution drove this group to terrorism. Its leader was Donald David DeFreeze (Cinque), an ex-con, and it was such a small group (10 or 12 members) that no one replaced DeFreeze after his death in a gun battle with police.

The SLA's first political move was the assassination of an Oakland school administrator, Marcus A. Foster, in November 1973. It was the kidnapping of Patricia Hearst, however, that gave the group national exposure. Hearst, whose father was the president and publisher of the *San Francisco Examiner*, gave the SLA publicity, especially after she converted to the cause. In a gun battle with the police on May 17, 1974, the leadership of the Symbionese Liberation Army was almost wiped out. The few survivors were captured in 1975, and they ended up with long prison terms. While the SLA no longer exists, it lives on in terrorist mythology.

Thunderbolt (al-Sa'iqa) (Syria)
This organization is the military wing of the Vanguards of the Popular War for the Liberation of Palestine. Founded in 1968 by Zuheir Mohsen, a former Syrian army officer, this group is pro-Syrian and its members are Ba'ath party members of Palestinian origin. Its activities were more directed for a pan-Arab revolution than for the establishment of a separate Palestinian state. The leadership envisaged Thunderbolt as an alternative to al-Fatah, and for years it was al-Fatah's chief rival. Mohsen was assassinated in 1979 by a rival Palestinian group, leading to speculation that al-Fatah was ridding itself of competition. Issam al-Qadi became the new leader. Its strength has been estimated at about 2,000 supporters, but with support from the Syrians in the mid-1970s, it recruited as many as 8,000 adherents. Although this group has been on record as opposing international terrorism, some of its members took a group of Soviet Jews hostage in Austria in 1973. This group is controlled so tightly by Syria that other Palestinian terrorist organizations distrust it.

Tupamaros-Movimiento de Liberacion Nacional (MLN) (Uruguay)
This urban guerilla group was one of the largest and most successful of the South American terrorist organizations. It took its name from the defeated Inca chief Tupac Amaru, who was executed by the Spanish in 1784 for his part in an Indian uprising. A group of Marxist rural partisans formed the organization in 1963, but they soon found more success as urban guerillas in Montevideo. Raul Sendic was the founder and most important leader of this movement.

At its peak in the early 1970s, Tupamaros attracted about 3,000 adherents. Its most famous terrorist act was the kidnapping and subsequent murder of a USAID public safety adviser, Daniel A. Mitrione. Several kidnappings and murders led the Uruguayan government to a military dictatorship in 1972. The counterterror was so successful that most of the leaders and followers are either dead or in prison. Despite their apparent success, the Tupamaros became more successful as a prototype of urban terrorists rather than as promoters of social revolution. Many of the European terrorist groups organized their followers into column formations based on the Tupamaros model.

Turkish People's Liberation Army (TPLA) (Turkey)
The TPLA was formed in the early 1970s with the goal of overthrowing the Turkish government. It has a Marxist-Maoist orientation and maintains

contacts with other left-wing organizations in Turkey and Europe. Its two principal leaders were Mahir Cayan and Deniz Gezmis, but they both were killed by Turkish security forces in the early 1970s. Estimates place its membership at about 300 activists, but it has numerous sympathizers. TPLA engaged in assassinations, bombings, kidnappings, and other antisocial activities during the 1970s. Its most famous terrorist act was the kidnapping and murder of Israel's consul general in Istanbul in May 1971. The Turkish military coup in 1980 has curtailed most of TPLA's terrorism as its leaders and members have emigrated or been arrested, killed, or executed.

Twenty-Sixth of July Movement (Cuba)
The Twenty-Sixth of July Movement was the official name of Fidel Castro's revolutionary group that overthrew the Batista regime in Cuba. Although this band of guerrillas fought mostly a traditional, low-intensity war against the Cuban armed forces, the movement did engage in several well-publicized terrorist acts. Several kidnappings and aircraft hijackings were conducted between 1956 and 1959. Once Castro seized power in January 1959, these terrorists incidents ceased. It was the success of this movement that led other Central and South American revolutionaries to adopt the same tactics, including terrorism.

Ulster Defence Association (UDA) (Northern Ireland)
The UDA is a Protestant terrorist group that fights to keep Ulster's close ties with Great Britain. It was founded in 1971 in direct response to an increase in IRA activity. Sammy Smyth was one of its founders, but other leaders soon came to the front. One such leader was Thomas Herron, a former hotel porter, but he was assassinated in September 1973. Other leaders have surfaced, including the current commander, Andy Tyrie. While Tyrie retains formal control of the UDA, political figures such as the Reverend Ian Paisley motivate the membership.

Most of the support for the UDA comes from the Protestant working class in Belfast. By far the most powerful paramilitary force in Northern Ireland, it has about 13,000 members with nearly 50,000 supporters. Despite UDA's official insistence on legality, it has conducted a terrorist campaign, including assassinations and revenge killings against Catholics suspected of IRA sympathies.

Ulster Freedom Fighters (UFF) (Northern Ireland)
This terrorist group is an offshoot of the Ulster Defence Association (UDA). UFF broke away from the UDA in 1973, and it has specialized

in random attacks against Catholic sympathizers of the IRA and IRA-Provos. While the UFF has always remained a small group, it has a reputation for carrying out assassinations that the UDA is reluctant to undertake. At least 11 murders have been attributed to the UFF, but recent inactivity may mean that this group has moderated its stance somewhat.

Warriors of Christ the King (Guerrilleros Del Christo Rey) (Spain)
This organization is a Spanish right-wing terrorist group built around religion. Its avowed purpose is to establish an international fascist alliance to fight against capitalism and communism. Mariano Sanchez Covisa is its leader. Members of this group have used assassinations, kidnappings, and beatings to advance their cause. This organization has considerable support in the Spanish army and the police. An attempted military coup by Lt. Col. Antonio Tejero in 1981 was also sponsored by this group. Any attempt by King Juan Carlos for liberalization and democracy is fought by this organization.

Weather Underground Organization (WUO) (United States)
This is the oldest terrorist group in the United States. It was founded in 1969 as a splinter group of the Students for a Democratic Society (SDS) by Mark Rudd and Bernardine Dohrn. At first this group was named the Weathermen, but the name was changed to the more gender-neutral Weather Underground Organization by Dohrn and feminist colleagues. Members of this organization advocated social revolution, but they were uncertain about how to bring it about.

Despite its limited numbers (probably only about a dozen active members), the Weather Underground may have been involved in nearly 500 terrorist incidents in 1969, particularly bombings and arson. A bomb accident in March 1970 killed seven of the group's top leaders, and their loss caused a lessening in the group's activities. Internal divisions resulting in a schism in the late 1970s further weakened this group. Some members surrendered to the authorities, but others went underground or joined other terrorist groups. The group surfaced again in 1981, committing a robbery in Nyack, New York, in which two policemen and a security guard were killed. After the arrest of Kathy Boudin for this robbery, the Weather Undergound ceased operations.

Wrath of God (Mivtzan Elohim) (Israel)
The Israeli intelligence service, the Mossad, created this group to carry out counterterrorist activities. Under its director, Major General

Aharon Yaviv, this group assassinated key Palestinian terrorist leaders. It was especially active during 1972–1973 in response to the terrorist incidents at the Munich Olympics and at various European and Israeli airports. They have assassinated at least six leaders of the Black September organization. The mistaken July 1973 assassination of a Moroccan waiter, Ahmed Bouchiki, as a leader in Black September and the resulting publicity ended the effectiveness of this group. Six members of the Wrath of God team were tried and sentenced to prison terms by the Norwegian authorities. While the Israeli intelligence service disbanded the Wrath of God in 1973, the proof of its former existence allowed Palestinian terrorist groups to claim Israeli responsibility for any violence directed toward Palestinian terrorists afterward.

6

Reference Materials

A CONSIDERABLE LITERATURE ON TERRORISM has emerged in the last 30 years. Before 1960, terrorism was considered only a limited threat against the international order and individual states, and the level of research interest was correspondingly low. The events of the 1960s changed conditions so much that terrorism came to be considered almost as important a threat to international stability as the rivalry between the United States and the Soviet Union. Suddenly, terrorism became a respectable line of academic study, and books and journal articles proliferated. Unfortunately, much of this research has proven to be ephemeral. Too often, however it has focused on preventive measures, rather than coming to grips with the nature and operation of terrorist organizations, as David Rapoport has pointed out in his introduction to *Inside Terrorist Organizations* (New York: Columbia University Press, 1988). Lacking an understanding of terrorism has hampered efforts to solve the problems that give rise to it. Also, because terrorism combines both politics and violence, it is difficult even for scholars to be objective. Consequently, the viewpoint of the author is often pronounced, and it influences the final product. This lack of objectivity in the literature on terrorism has been more harmful than in other fields because it has resulted in misinterpretation of the motives and actions of the various terrorist organizations. Considerable effort has been made in the following bibliography to point out any specific viewpoint and bias of the authors. The following is a selective bibliography of the best works available for a study of terrorism.

Selected Bibliography

Failing, Susan J., comp. **Terrorism, Guerrilla Warfare, Counterinsurgency, Low-Intensity Conflict and Revolutions.** Colorado Springs, CO: United States Air Force Academy Library, 1986. 99p.

Despite the fact that this bibliography was compiled for the U.S. Air Force Academy Library, it covers most of the literature on terrorism and guerrilla warfare published between 1976 and 1986. This book is organized around subject and geographic areas for ease of use. Unfortunately, subject and author indexes have been left out of this otherwise useful tool.

Global Terrorism: A Historical Bibliography. Santa Barbara, CA: ABC-CLIO, 1986. 168p. ISBN 0-87436-453-1.

This bibliography on international terrorism contains 598 abstracts and citations of journal articles gathered from ABC-CLIO's history database. While this book is organized in a somewhat unwieldy regional format, subject and author indexes make the citations more accessible. With three- to four-sentence citations, the user is able to judge both the subject matter and the scope of each cited work. This bibliography is a good way to gain access to difficult-to-reach journal articles.

Lakos, Amos. **International Terrorism: A Bibliography.** Boulder, CO: Westview, 1986. 481p. ISBN 0-8133-7157-0.

All books, articles, and documents on international terrorism in English are listed in this bibliography. Both the coverage and accuracy of the citations are excellent, and it has author and subject indexes for ease of use. Despite the lack of annotations, this bibliography is the best of its type on the market.

Lakos, Amos. **Terrorism, 1980–1990: A Bibliography.** Boulder, CO: Westview, 443p. ISBN 0-8133-8035-9

The author continues his efforts to achieve bibliographic control of the literature on terrorism and political violence. This work extends the scope of his earlier work to the period from 1980 to 1990. It provides a comprehensive listing of English-language materials published during the decade. Lakos is a librarian at the University of Waterloo in Ontario, Canada, and his efforts to provide access to materials on terrorism and political violence have proved beneficial to both the specialist and the amateur.

Mickolus, Edward F., comp. **The Literature of Terrorism: A Selectively Annotated Bibliography.** Westport, CT: Greenwood, 1980. 553p. ISBN 0-313-22265-7.

This is still one of the best bibliographical sources on terrorism around, with comprehensive coverage of periodical literature in the 1970s. The author has subdivided the material into numerous categories including sections on tactics, philosophies, geographic area, and responses. This book is unique in that it was reviewed by the Central Intelligence Agency's Publication Review Board since the author was once affiliated with that agency.

Norton, Augustus R., and Martin H. Greenberg. **International Terrorism: An Annotated Bibliography and Research Guide.** Boulder, CO: Westview, 1980. ISBN 0-89158-461-7.

The authors attempt to establish bibliographic control over the literature on terrorism and to provide guidance on research in the field. Annotations are uneven in quality and much material is noted as unseen, but despite these faults, this bibliography should be consulted because the authors have found materials missed in other bibliographies. It is also strong on theoretical works on terrorism.

Smith, Myron J. **The Secret Wars: A Guide to Sources in English: Vol. III, International Terrorism, 1968–1980.** Santa Barbara, CA: ABC-CLIO, 1980. 237p. ISBN 0-87436-304-7.

English-language materials on international terrorism appearing from 1968 to 1980 have been collected in this useful bibliography. Books, articles, documents, papers, and reports are included under each subject heading. Another feature is a breakdown of the materials by country of origin. The author has covered the materials on terrorism in the period from 1968 to 1980 in depth, and this bibliography will always remain an excellent source for researchers.

Annuals

Jaffee Center for Strategic Studies Project on Terrorism. **INTER: A Review of International Terrorism.** Jerusalem: Jaffee Center for Strategic Studies Project on Terrorism. Annual. $22.50. ISSN 86-645044.

The Jaffee Center for Strategic Studies' Project on Terrorism has surveyed international terrorism each year since 1984. Statistical data on terrorist activities and brief articles on terrorist trends are contained in each annual. Other useful features are a chronology of significant international terrorist events and a glossary of terrorist organizations. This report is the best available source on terrorism in the Middle East.

Scherer, John L., ed. **Terrorism: An Annual Survey.** Minneapolis, MN: John L. Scherer. Annual. 1982–1983. ISSN 0278-66X.

This annual provides a listing of terrorist activities throughout the world for the years 1982 and 1983. Besides citations of terrorist incidents, it contains a list of the major terrorist groups by country active in the early 1980s. While this annual promised more than it could deliver and ceased publication in 1983, it is a useful source because of its statistical treatment of terrorism.

U.S. Department of State. **Patterns of Global Terrorism.** Washington, DC. Annual.

Each year, the U.S. State Department produces a summary of international terrorist activity. These booklets contain charts, graphs, and statistical material on terrorist acts. Particularly valuable are the sections with regional breakdowns of terrorist incidents and the charts on terrorist incidents during the previous five years. This annual is one of the most up-to-date sources on international terrorist activities available anywhere.

Databooks, Handbooks, and Sourcebooks

Alexander, Yonah, Marjorie Ann Browne, and Allen S. Nanes, eds. **Control of Terrorism: International Documents.** New York: Crane Russak, 1979. 212p. ISBN 0-8448-1327-3.

This sourcebook contains documents dealing with international efforts to control terrorism in the twentieth century. Major treaties, international and regional treaties, and resolutions by both the United Nations (UN) and the International Civil Aviation Organization (ICAO) are highlighted. This book brings major and minor antiterrorism agreements into a single volume for the benefit of the specialist and the student of terrorism.

Alexander, Yonah, and Allan S. Nanes, eds. **Legislative Responses to Terrorism.** Dordrecht, The Netherlands: Martinus Nijhoff, 1986. 327p. ISBN 90-247-3213-1.

This sourcebook presents selected national legislation on terrorism and political violence from English-language countries. After a brief introduction on the history of antiterrorism legislation, the legal codes of 18 countries are listed. These legal texts are easy to use, and this sourcebook constitutes a valuable tool for researchers.

Bassiouni, M. Cherif. **International Crimes: Digest/Index of International Instruments, 1915–1985.** 2 vols. New York: Oceana, 1986. ISBN 0-379-20139-9.

This two-volume sourcebook on legal documents and agreements on international crimes since 1815 is an invaluable reference work. These volumes cover such offenses as territorial aggression, war crimes, unlawful use of weapons, crimes against humanity, genocide, racial discrimination, slavery, piracy, aircraft hijacking, and hostage-taking of civilians. This sourcebook has a place in any reference collection on international security.

Bolz, Frank, Kenneth J. Dudonis, and David P. Schulz. **The Counter-Terrorism Handbook: Tactics, Procedures, and Techniques.** New York: Elsevier, 1990. 233p. ISBN 0-444-01524-8.

Three American authors with backgrounds in law enforcement and journalism have combined their experiences to write a manual on counterterrorism. They have organized the book into three distinct sections: "Pre-incident," "Incident," and "Post-incident." Their thesis is that terrorism is here to stay and that the American public must be prepared to cope with it in a practical manner. The virtue of this handbook is its methodical law enforcement approach toward countering terrorism.

Dobson, Christopher, and Ronald Payne. **The Terrorists: Their Weapons, Leaders and Tactics.** New York: Facts on File, 1982. Revised ed. 262p. ISBN 0-87196-669-7.

The authors survey both public and informal sources to analyze terrorism and terrorists. No other source covers the topic of terrorist leadership in as much depth, and its who's who of terrorism gives much valuable background on terrorist leaders. It also provides useful information on funding, training, weapons, and tactics.

Friedlander, Robert A. **Terrorism: Documents of International and Local Control.** 5 vols. London: Oceana, 1979–1990. ISBN 0-379-00690-1.

While this series started out as a selective representation of the legal and societal aspects of international terrorism, the growth of terrorism resulted in the author compiling a five-volume set. Government documents, UN reports, international legal cases, and Council of Europe papers are all reproduced here. This is one of the most complete collections of documents on international terrorism available.

Gurr, Ted Robert. **Handbook of Political Conflict: Theory and Research.** New York: Free Press, 1980. 566p. ISBN 0-02-912760-2.

A generation of theoretical and empirical research on the origins, process, and consequences of political conflict is surveyed in this handbook. The author defines political conflict to include political riots, insurrection, revolution, terrorism, and war. Terrorism constitutes only a small part of this study, but the essays are of such high quality that this book should be included in any collection on terrorism.

Illich, Richard B. **Transnational Terrorism: Conventions and Commentary: A Compilation of Treaties, Agreements and Declarations of Especial Interest to the United States.** Charlottesville, VA: Michie, 1982. 281p. ISBN 0-87-215494-7.

Legal agreements, negotiated treaties, and unilateral declarations on international terrorism are the documents contained in this invaluable sourcebook. The author is a legal scholar at the University of Virginia who gathered source materials on terrorism beginning in the late 1960s. Among the special features are documents on past efforts to control terrorism, proposed conventions, and lists of countries ratifying terrorist agreements.

Israeli, Raphael, ed. **PLO in Lebanon: Selected Documents.** New York: St. Martin's, 1983. 316p. ISBN 0-312-59381-3.

These documents were captured from the Palestine Liberation Organization (PLO) by Israeli military forces in June 1982. In its invasion the Israeli Defense Force (IDF) captured dozens of PLO base camps and seized confidential correspondence. The Israelis have released the contents of some of the documents in this book in English translation along with the original Arabic texts. While this book has been edited by Israeli authorities, it does give insight into the operations and the philosophy behind the PLO.

Mickolus, Edward F. **Transnational Terrorism: A Chronology of Events, 1968–1979.** Westport, CT: Greenwood, 1980. 967p. ISBN 0-313-222-6-1.

The author presents a detailed chronology of international terrorist incidents during 1968–1979. These incidents form the data for the author's International Terrorism: Attributes of Terrorist Events (IT-ERATE) computer system. Although most of the material deals with terrorist organizations, state-sponsored terrorism is also treated in some depth. This book has a mass of material invaluable for retrospective studies on international terrorism.

Mickolus, Edward F., Todd Sandler, and Jean M. Murdock. **International Terrorism in the 1980s: A Chronology of Events.** Vol. 1. Ames: Iowa State University Press, 1989. ISBN 0-8138-0024-2.

The authors have produced the first volume of an effort to continue Mickolus's earlier chronology of terrorist activity, *Transnational Terrorism.* This volume covers terrorist activity during 1980–1983, with the promise that subsequent volumes will cover the rest of the 1980s. Although the organization differs slightly, the comprehensiveness of the earlier work and its dependence on ITERATE are continued in this volume. This sourcebook will remain the standard work of its type for at least the next decade.

Seger, Karl A. **The Antiterrorism Handbook: A Practical Guide to Counteraction Planning and Operations for Individuals, Businesses, and Government.** Novato, CA: Presidio, 1990. 230p. ISBN 0-89141-369-3.

The author, a veteran of countless training sessions on counterterrorism techniques, disseminates his findings in this handbook. He provides insights on what to do and what to avoid in dealing with terrorism. His checklists in the appendixes are especially valuable because they have been tested by him over time. This book is one of the most up-to-date handbooks on counterterrorism available.

U.S. House of Representatives, Committee on Foreign Affairs staff, eds. **International Terrorism: A Compilation of Major Laws, Treaties, Agreements, and Executive Documents.** Washington, DC: U.S. Government Printing Office, 1987. 970p.

Most of the significant laws, treaties, bilateral and multilateral agreements, and executive branch documents are contained in this useful sourcebook. It was prepared for the use of the Committee on Foreign Affairs for its deliberations on antiterrorism legislation, and it includes statistics on terrorism involving U.S. nationals for the year 1985. It is most useful as a quick source for documents on the official U.S. policy toward terrorism during the Reagan administration.

Directories

Andrade, John M. **World Police and Paramilitary Forces.** New York: Stockton, 1985.

This directory contains detailed information on the world's police and paramilitary forces capable of combating terrorism. Each country's police, internal security, paramilitary, and private security organizations are outlined along with estimates of the size of each force. Most of this information was gathered by the author when he was connected with major intelligence organizations.

Janke, Peter. **Guerrilla and Terrorist Organizations: A World Directory and Bibliography.** New York: Macmillan, 1983. 531p. ISBN 0-02916-150-9.

Direct action organizations and political movements that have posed a threat to established governments since World War II are listed in this directory. The author first surveys the topic in seven geographical regions and then lists each guerrilla and terrorist group in alphabetical order by country. An index provides helpful access.

Rosie, George. **The Directory of International Terrorism.** New York: Paragon House, 1987. 310p. ISBN 0-913729-29-9.

Each citation in this directory of terrorists and terrorist activity over the last two centuries is a comprehensive analysis of each organization, person, and/or event based on the most recent material available. This book is the best retrospective reference work on terrorism available.

Schmid, Alex P. **Political Terrorism: A Research Guide to Concepts, Theories, Data Bases and Literature.** Amsterdam: North-Holland, 1983. 585p. ISBN 0-4448-5602-1.

This volume provides the basic definitions, conceptual frameworks, and bibliographic sources for the study of political terrorism. Among its special features is a country-by-country listing of terrorist organizations and a lengthy bibliography of works on political terrorism. The section on databases and database construction in the field of terrorism is another notable feature. Recommended, although some of the material is beginning to become dated.

Encyclopedias

Sifakis, Carl. **The Encyclopedia of Assassinations.** New York: Facts on File, 1991. 228 pp ISBN 0-8160-1935-5.

The author uses this encyclopedia to survey political assassinations throughout history. Many of the assassinations are outside the scope of modern terrorism, but approximately a third of the citations concern political figures since 1945. Each citation is lengthy and illustrations are a useful addition. This book is a popular treatment of the subject, but the author gives a valuable look at the history of political assassinations.

Thackrah, John Richard. **Encyclopedia of Terrorism and Political Violence.** London: Routledge and Kegan Paul, 1987. 308 pp. ISBN 0-7102-0659-3.

This British encyclopedia by an instructor at the Police Staff College, London, intends to fill an information gap in terrorist literature by bringing together the most recent research on terrorism and political violence. Ideas, theories, and terms interest the author most, but there is also information on individual groups and incidents. Although an antiterrorism bias on the part of the author is apparent, this short encyclopedia provides much useful information on modern terrorism for both the scholar and the general reader.

Wilson, Colin, and Donald Seaman. **The Encyclopedia of Modern Murder, 1962–1982.** New York: Putnam, 1983. 279p. ISBN 0-399-12983-9.

Murderers of all types, from psychopaths to terrorists, are included in this concise encyclopedia. Each citation has an essay on the life and crimes of the criminal, or a short history of the terrorist organization responsible. The sections on terrorists and terrorist organizations are very useful. This book is a good background source for those interested in starting research on terrorists and terrorism.

Government Hearings and Reports

U.S. Department of Defense. **Report of the DOD Commission on Beirut International Airport Terrorist Act, October 23, 1983.** Washington, DC: Department of Defense, 1983. 141p.

This report contains the official findings of the Department of Defense on the October 23, 1983 suicide bombing attack on U.S. forces in Beirut. Five former and present senior military officers surveyed the background and the incident itself. The weakness of the survey is in its gathering and interpretation of intelligence information, but the report shows clearly how mistakes were made that ultimately endangered the Marines. This report appeared only two months after the bombing, and it has been criticized as a rush to judgment.

U.S. House of Representatives, Committee on Foreign Affairs. **Impact of International Terrorism on Travel.** Washington, DC: U.S. Government Printing Office, 1986. 432p.

Two congressional subcommittees considered testimony and statements from witnesses over the state of security at international airports. Most of the witnesses testified that international airport security had improved, but American travelers were still at risk. Controversy erupted between representatives of the tourist industry and safety experts over the risks American tourists faced in traveling to Europe at the time. These hearings on terrorist activities at international airports produced much useful data on terrorism.

U.S. House of Representatives, Committee on Foreign Affairs. **International Terrorism: 1985.** Washington, DC: U.S. Government Printing Office, 1985. 339p.

This is a record of congressional hearings called to review the effectiveness of the Anti-Terrorism Training Assistance Program and the operation of the Office for Counter-Terrorism and Emergency Planning, which provide security for diplomats and diplomatic facilities. There is also information here about counterterrorist activities. The hearings and the supporting documents are useful in gauging government steps to counter international terrorism.

U.S. Senate, Committee on the Judiciary. **Legal Mechanisms to Combat Terrorism.** Washington, DC: U.S. Government Printing Office, 1986. 332p.

This is the record of hearings held in April 1986 to study possible civil and criminal actions against the PLO. The testimony and supporting documents were hostile toward Yasser Arafat and the PLO, yet the committee did not resolve the problem of how to bring civil or criminal proceedings against them. This hearing produced a mass of assertions about PLO terrorist activities, but supporting evidence was lacking.

U.S. Senate, Committee on the Judiciary. **State-Sponsored Terrorism.** Washington, DC: U.S. Government Printing Office, 1985. 186p.

This report on state-sponsored terrorism was commissioned by the Senate Subcommittee on Security and Terrorism to augment hearings on international terrorism scheduled for the spring of 1985. Authors Ray S. Cline and Yonah Alexander, both experts on international terrorism, had support from the subcommittee staff. The report identifies states suspected of actively exporting terrorism in the mid-1980s: the Soviet Union, Iran, Libya, and Syria. This report recommends "a coherent and firm U.S. policy on responding to state-sponsored terrorism with effective countermeasures" that could win public understanding and support.

U.S. Senate, Committee on the Judiciary. **Terrorism and Security: The Italian Experience.** Washington, DC: U.S. Government Printing Office, 1984. 94p.

This report includes updated versions of *A Study of the Restructure of Italian Intelligence and Security Services* (1978), and *Contemporary Italian Terrorism: Analysis and Countermeasures* (1979) by Vittorfranco S. Pisano, which assess the efforts of Italian antiterrorist forces.

Journals

Terrorism
John L. Scherer
4900 18th Avenue
Minneapolis, MN 55417
612-723-2947
1982– . Quarterly. $45. ISSN 0278-663X.

This journal replaced *Terrorism: An Annual Survey*. It is edited and published by John L. Scherer, who has made a lifelong study of terrorism. It specializes in information and statistics on terrorism with special emphasis on surveys of terrorist activities and biographies of terrorists. This is the best place to find statistical information on terrorism.

Terrorism: An International Journal
Taylor and Francis
1900 Frost Road, Suite 101
Bristol, PA 19007
1977– . Quarterly, $110. ISSN 0149-0389.

This bimonthly publication serves as a forum for the study of the theory and practice of terrorism. The format alternates between special issues on specific topics and open issues. Special features are book reviews, documents, and statistics on terrorism.

Terrorism and Political Violence
Frank Cass
Gainesborough House
11 Gainesborough Rd.
London E11 1RS
081-530-4226
1989– . Quarterly. $40. ISSN 0954-6553

A new addition to the journal literature on terrorism, this British quarterly is edited by two leading authorities on terrorism, David C. Rapoport and Paul Wilkinson. It offers an academic study of all aspects of terrorism and political violence. Besides solid scholarly articles, this journal specializes in book reviews. It serves as the scholarly counterpart in Europe to the American journal *Terrorism: An International Journal*.

TVI Report: Comprehensively Reporting Terrorism, Violence, Insurgency Worldwide
TVI
Box 1055
Beverly Hills, CA 90210
213-276-3378
1979- . Quarterly. $70.

This publication, formerly the *TVI Journal,* contains articles on all aspects of international terrorism and violence, mostly short features on specific terrorist topics. Sections on recent terrorist incidents and book reviews make this journal useful for both beginning and advanced researchers on terrorism and violence.

Textbooks and Juvenile-Level Works

Bender, David L., and Bruno Leone. **Terrorism: Opposing Viewpoints.** St. Paul, MN: Greenhaven, 1986. 240p. ISBN 0-89908-389-7.

Various opinions on the nature and justification of terrorism have been brought together in this book. While all of these articles have appeared in other publications, the juxtaposition of diverse arguments makes this a unique source. Bibliographies of books and periodicals are also a useful feature of this book. This publication is most valuable for stimulating classroom discussion about terrorism.

Freeman, Charles. **Terrorism.** London: Batsford, 1981. 72p. ISBN 0-7134-1230-5.

This brief book deals with all aspects of terrorism, defined by the author as the use of fear as a weapon to achieve political ends. The analysis and illustrations make this book appropriate for high-school coursework. The information is sufficiently current, and the book serves well as a useful introduction to the study of terrorism.

Friedlander, Robert A. **Terror-Violence: Aspects of Social Control.** London: Oceana Publications, 1983. 299p. ISBN 0-379-20748-6.

This textbook on international terrorism and its impact on western democratic institutions is designed to be used in conjunction with the author's *Terrorism: Documents of International and Local Control.* Constant reference is made to documents in the course of surveying the theory and practice of international terrorism. This textbook is intended primarily for undergraduate and graduate level college coursework.

Harris, Jonathan. **The New Terrorism: Politics of Violence.** New York: Julian Messner, 1983. 197p. ISBN 0-671-45807-8.

The dynamics of modern international terrorism are examined in this textbook. All aspects of international terrorism are analyzed, from training to the commission of a terrorist act. Counterterrorism strategies are also studied in this survey. This book is an excellent source on the topic to include in the social studies section of the library at the junior and senior high school levels.

Poland, James. **Understanding Terrorism: Groups, Strategies, and Responses.** Englewood Cliffs, NJ: Prentice Hall, 1988.

This up-to-date and knowledgeable source avoids some of the common biases in terrorism studies by balancing the proterrorism and antiterrorism viewpoints. One strength is the list of questions at the end of each chapter.

Microforms

Davis, Michael. ed.; Mike Acquaviva, comp. **A Guide to Terrorism, Special Studies, 1975–1985.** 5 microfilm reels. Frederick, MD: University Publications of America, 1986.

This microfilm set contains a number of significant short studies on terrorism produced by government agencies and by think tanks under government contract. Several of the Rand Foundation studies are of special importance because of their statistical data.

Monographs on Terrorism

Philosophy and Theory of Terrorism

Alexander, Yonah, and John M. Gleason, eds. **Behavioral and Quantitative Perspectives on Terrorism.** New York: Pergamon, 1981. 393p. ISBN 0-08-025989-8.

This book of essays examines the behavioral and quantitative approaches to an analysis of terrorism. These papers are an outgrowth of a joint meeting of the Operations Research Society of America and the Institute of Management Sciences in New York in 1978. The result is a book with a variety of theoretical approaches to the study of terrorism. Both the quality of its papers and the theoretical concepts behind the research make this book a good place to look for insights into the terrorism outbreak of the late 1970s.

Burton, Anthony M. **Urban Terrorism: Theory, Practice and Response.** New York: Free Press, 1975. 259p.

A classic study of the theory and practice of urban terrorism. Other books have dealt with this subject but not in as much depth or with as much understanding of the urban guerrilla.

Chaliand, Gerard. **Terrorism: From Popular Struggle to Media Spectacle.** Atlantic Highlands, NJ: Saqi Books, 1987. ISBN 0-8635-6168-3.

The author, a French expert, concludes that terrorism is merely another weapon of revolutionary guerrillas in their campaign of psychological warfare. Terrorism is a natural outgrowth of the anti-colonial struggle, which has merged into the movement of wars of liberation. However, terrorism has not been as successful as guerrilla warfare because it has generated more publicity than political change. This book ties the guerrilla and terrorist traditions together in a highly stimulating work.

Crenshaw, Martha, ed. **Terrorism, Legitimacy and Power: The Consequences of Political Violence.** Middletown, CT: Wesleyan University Press, 1983. 162p. ISBN 0-8195-5081-7.

These essays deal with the threat of terrorism against states, societies, and individuals in the West. The papers are a product of a symposium on terrorism held at Wesleyan University in 1982. Authors contend that governments must learn to adapt to terrorism because it is likely to become a permanent feature of politics among and within nations. These essays consider terrorism in a variety of different settings.

Dobson, Christopher, and Ronald Payne. **The Never-Ending War: Terrorism in the 80s.** New York: Facts on File, 1987. 356p. ISBN 0-8160-1537-6.

Two experts update the status of terrorism through 1986, including previously unpublished information about the groups.

Freedman, Lawrence Zelic, and Yonah Alexander, eds. **Perspectives on Terrorism.** Wilmington, DE: Scholarly Resources, 1983. 254p. ISBN 0-8420-2201-5.

These essays cover a variety of perspectives on terrorist activities, from skyjacking to nuclear terrorism. The authors emphasize the psychological dimensions of terrorism and profile individual terrorists. Several sections also are devoted to hostage-taking situations and counterterrorism tactics. This book is a comprehensive look at terrorism from a variety of viewpoints.

Gutteridge, William, ed. **Contemporary Terrorism.** New York: Facts on File, 1986. 225p. ISBN 0-8160-1468-X.

This compilation of British and European writings on contemporary trends in terrorism was sponsored by the Institute for the Study of Conflict, London. It is organized into two sections: one studies the terrorist threat to democratic institutions, and the other looks at recent terrorist activity in France, Italy, Spain, and West Germany. All of the authors are recognized authorities on terrorism. This book provides a good look at terrorism in the mid-1980s. The early chapters on the threat of terrorism to the Western democracies are especially valuable.

Han, Henry Hyunwook, ed. **Terrorism, Political Violence and World Order.** Lanham, MD: University Press of America, 1984. 767p. ISBN 0-8191-3740-5.

These 43 papers come from a three-day seminar on international terrorism and political violence at Central Michigan University in 1982 and from invited contributions from other scholars. The result is a potpourri of opinions and information on terrorist activities during the late 1970s and early 1980s. The diversity of views represented by the authors is noteworthy. This book is a mine of information, but difficult to use because the topics are loosely organized.

Hanle, Donald. **Terrorism: The Newest Face of Warfare.** Washington, DC: Pergamon-Brasseys International Defense Publishers, 1989. 254p. ISBN 0-08-036742-9.

A career U.S. Air Force officer gives a new twist to the theory of terrorism by advancing the thesis that terrorism is a form of war based upon the manipulation of force to meet political objectives. He concludes that, with the exception of state terrorism, all forms of terrorism employ force as a form of war. Counterterrorist policies must be attuned to this principle before counterterrorism can succeed. This book provides a unique look at terrorism by placing it in a military context.

Laqueur, Walter. **The Age of Terrorism.** Boston: Little, Brown, 1987. 385p. ISBN 0-316-51478-0.

This book is an update of the author's earlier work, *Terrorism* (1977), but it is more a summation of an eminent scholar's ideas on terrorism's role in modern society than a revision of his earlier book. The author examines terrorism in detail and concludes that terrorism has failed to overthrow any government or regime. Terrorism has superseded guerrilla warfare, but it has made no lasting contributions except terror.

Merkl, Peter H., ed. **Political Violence and Terror: Motifs and Motivations.** Berkeley: University of California Press, 1986. 380p. ISBN 0-520-05605-1.

This collection of essays studies methodological and psychological aspects of political violence and terrorism. Most of the authors devote their attention to European terrorist groups, but Latin American and Middle Eastern organizations are also surveyed. The emphasis is on clarifying the relationship between ideology and violent action rather than listings of terrorist incidents. This book contains some of the more original studies of terrorism around.

Mommsen, Wolfgang J., and Gerhard Hirschfeld, eds. **Social Protest, Violence and Terror in Nineteenth- and Twentieth-Century Europe.** London: Berg, 1982. 411p. ISBN 0-333-32002-6.

The antecedents of modern terrorism are studied in this historical treatment of political violence and terror in nineteenth- and early twentieth-century Europe. Specialists on political violence contributed essays on the major activist movements during this period. They indicate that modern terrorism is different from the earlier movements but only in ideology or specific cause, not in tactics or general philosophy. This book is a solid effort with high-quality essays and a good concluding piece.

Morgan, Robin. **The Demon Lover: On the Sexuality of Terrorism.** New York: Norton, 1989. 395p. ISBN 0-393-02642-6.

This book is a feminist analysis of terrorism by a prominent American scholar. The author draws a psychological profile of terrorists, and presents results of interviews with women terrorists and women in the refugee camps of the Middle East. The unusual interpretation of the behavior of terrorists contributes to the understanding of terrorism.

O'Sullivan, Noel, ed. **Terrorism, Ideology, and Revolution.** Boulder, CO: Westview, 1986. 232p. ISBN 0-8133-0345-1.

Nine British scholars on terrorism contributed essays here on the historical development of terrorism and its modern form. They conclude that terrorism in its modern form is a European phenomenon, but recent developments show that terrorism has expanded into its international phase. Terrorism is studied in its Islamic, Irish, Latin American, and Turkish derivatives. The authors have managed to combine political theory, political science, and history into a comprehensive study of modern terrorism.

Parry, Albert. **Terrorism from Robespierre to Arafat.** New York: Vanguard, 1976. 624p. ISBN 0-8149-0746-6.

An American scholar presents a history of terrorism from its beginnings to its modern variants. While the author rejects all forms of terrorism, he admits that it has a long historical record. His sections on nineteenth- and early twentieth-century terrorism are the strength of the book, as they place modern terrorism in a historical context. This book is a solid addition to background reading on terrorism, but other works need to be consulted to understand modern terrorist movements.

Purcell, Hugh. **Revolutionary War: Guerrilla Warfare and Terrorism in Our Time.** London: Hamish Hamilton, 1980. 96p. ISBN 0-241-10331-2.

Revolutionary war and its derivatives are the subject of this short book. The author defines revolutionary war as any sudden and violent attempt to win power. According to his definition, terrorism occurs when there are not enough revolutionaries to form a guerrilla army and they are too weak to challenge the state's military forces. While this book is almost too eclectic in its look at revolutions, wars of liberation, and terrorism, it still serves as a good introduction to these topics.

Rapoport, David C., and Yonah Alexander, eds. **The Morality of Terrorism: Religious and Secular Justifications.** New York: Pergamon, 1982. 377p. ISBN 0-08-026347.

The historical and moral justification for terrorist activity are the subjects of this book of essays by American, British, and Israeli specialists on terrorism. Special emphasis is placed on "the moral climate that produces terrorism, the doctrines terrorists use to justify themselves, and the moral predicaments terrorists create." The quality of these 15 essays is of such a high level that this is one of the more significant books on terrorism published in the early 1980s.

Rapoport, David C., and Yonah Alexander, eds. **The Rationalization of Terrorism.** Frederick, MD: University Publications of America, 1982. 233p. ISBN 0-89093-413-4

Explanations and rationalizations for terrorist behavior are the subjects of these papers from a conference on international terrorism at UCLA in March 1979. Most of the papers emphasize the dilemma of terrorists who want to arouse moral outrage and sympathy for their cause and not simply terror. Both the papers and the discussions point out that terrorism usually inspires outrage among the intended audience rather than sympathy. This book succeeds somewhat in a difficult task: to explain terrorism from the Western democratic viewpoint.

Rubenstein, Richard E. **Alchemists of Revolution: Terrorism in the Modern World.** New York: Basic Books, 1987. 266p. ISBN 0-465-00095-9.

An American academic provides a thoughtful analysis of terrorism and its place in modern politics. He concludes that terrorism can only be understood by recognizing the alienation of politicized young adults from society. Counterterrorism policy remains ineffectual because no government has been able to develop and maintain a consistent counterterrorist strategy. This book is difficult reading, but its reward is a much better insight into the psychology of terrorism.

Santoro, Victor. **Disruptive Terrorism.** Port Townsend, WA: Loopanics Unlimited, 1984. 135p. ISBN 0-915179-17-2.

The author treats the possible scenarios of a small group of terrorists practicing disruptive terrorism. Disruptive terrorism is where a number of related violent incidents orchestrated by terrorists come together to either interrupt normal business or provide unwelcome and damaging publicity. The author believes that this type of terrorism has more potential than destructive terrorism, such as bombings and assassinations, because it is so hard to control. This book is a close look at a unique type of terrorism.

Segaller, Stephen. **Invisible Armies: Terrorism into the 1990s.** San Diego: Harcourt Brace Jovanovich, 1987. 310p. ISBN 0-15-145288-1.

A British TV journalist used his experience on a British documentary series called "Terror" to write this book on terrorism. His thesis is that pragmatism must replace dogmatism in understanding and countering terrorism. A chapter on the *Achille Lauro* incident illustrates this point most effectively since political considerations became more important in that case than antiterrorism policy. While this book is a popular treatment of terrorism, its viewpoints make it a good introduction for further study.

Stohl, Michael, ed. **The Politics of Terrorism.** 2d ed. New York: Marcel Dekker, 1983. 473p. ISBN 0-8247-1908-5.

The theories, concepts, strategies, and ideologies of political terrorism are examined in this revised edition of an earlier work. These essays range from studies of random violence to state-sponsored terrorism, but the theme emerges that terrorism must be understood in its sociopolitical setting. Rather than blaming terrorism on the former Soviet Union, the authors try to understand it in its international context. This book is a good introduction to the concepts and the practices of terrorism.

Taylor, Maxwell. **The Terrorists.** London: Brassey's Defence Publishers, 1988. 205p. ISBN 0-08-033603-5.

A British psychologist studied individual terrorists and terrorist groups for clues to terrorist behavior. He concludes that concepts such as the terrorist personality have little usefulness and make it more difficult to understand terrorism. It is in the study of group allegiance and interaction where the best chance of understanding terrorism resides. This book is both stimulating and difficult to read, but it will remain the best source on terrorist behavior.

Wardlaw, Grant. **Political Terrorism: Theory, Tactics, and Counter-Measures.** 2d ed. Cambridge: Cambridge University Press, 1989. 248p. ISBN 0-521-25032-3.

The author intends this book to outline the policy considerations that a democratic state confronts in combating terrorism. He claims that terrorism is a more effective threat in the modern political environment than in the past because communications, weapons, and the social structure make modern society more vulnerable. While modern terrorist groups have been relatively conservative and repetitive in their actions, there is no certainty that terrorists will not seize more spectacular and dangerous weapons in the future. This book offers a bleak look at terrorist trends, but it is based on solid research and sound conclusions.

Warner, Martin, and Roger Crisp, eds. **Terrorism, Protest and Power.** Aldershot, England: Edward Elgar, 1990. 197p. ISBN 1-85278-202-1.

These essays on the philosophy and practice of terrorism were prepared under the auspices of the Society for Applied Philosophy. Each of the authors takes a perspective on the ethical or philosophical underpinnings of terrorism (e.g., whether to call them terrorists or freedom fighters). Of special significance to the authors is the relationship between political opposition to the state and the final resort to terrorism. Some of these essays are tough reading, but the effort is rewarding in understanding the ethical and philosophical background of terrorism.

Wilkinson, Paul. **Terrorism and the Liberal State.** New York: New York University Press, 1986. 2d ed. 322p. ISBN 0-333-39490-9.

A British expert surveys the dilemmas of democratic societies having to deal with terrorism. His conclusion is that democracies can take measures to defend society against terrorism without putting basic civil liberties and political democracy at risk. The prime concern is that the state not overreact and launch repressive countermeasures. At the same time, it is not advisable to appease terrorists. The author argues that the Western democracies should pursue a moderate course between the extremes.

Zimmermann, Ekkart. **Political Violence, Crises, and Revolutions: Theories and Research.** Boston: G. K. Hall, 1983. 792p. ISBN 0-8161-9027-5.

This book studies antigovernment and antisystem violence occurring within a political system. While international terrorism is not addressed directly, the recurrent conditions that contribute to an understanding of terrorism are studied in depth. Most of the analysis involves a cross-national approach to the fields of political violence, crises, and revolution. This massive study of political violence provides the readers of both international security and terrorism an invaluable background source.

State-Sponsored Terrorism

Chomsky, Noam. **Pirates and Emperors: International Terrorism in the Real World.** New York: Claremont Research and Publications, 1986. 174p. ISBN 0912439-07-6.

A prominent American academic critic of state terrorism uses this book to expose inconsistency in the U.S. stance on terrorism. He accuses the United States of a double standard in attacking other countries and organizations for promoting terrorist activities when the U.S. government also conducts terrorist operations. This double standard allows the U.S. government to preach against international terrorism while at the same time sponsoring terrorism against selected targets. Though controversial, this viewpoint is shared by many in the Third World.

George, Alexander, ed. **Western State Terrorism.** New York: Routledge, 1991. 264 pp. ISBN 0-415-90472-2.

These essays, mostly by American academics, discuss the extent to which Western states use terrorism to advance their political interests. Four examples of state terrorism—American counterinsurgent state terrorism, British terrorism in Northern Ireland, Indonesia's use of state terrorism, and the state terrorism policies in southern Africa—are examined for lessons. The thesis is that the United States and its client states have been the major sponsors of terrorism in the world for the last twenty years. This book is a radical treatment of state terrorism.

International Security Council. **State Terrorism and the International System.** New York: CAUSA Publications, 1986. 114p.

This book includes nine essays from a 1986 conference of national security advisers from 12 nations, held in Tel Aviv. Both the formal declaration of the conference and the conclusion of the papers is that the Soviet Union was the principal sponsor of international terrorism. These papers are more statements on terrorism than works of scholarship, but the viewpoints from a variety of statesmen and scholars in the field are noteworthy.

Schamis, Gerardo Jorge. **War and Terrorism in International Affairs.** New Brunswick, NJ: Transaction Books, 1980. 89p. ISBN 0-87855-808-X.

This book assesses the characteristics of international terrorism. The author argues that terrorism now constitutes a new form of warfare that has been sponsored by underdeveloped countries to fight against militarily stronger countries. It has also been adopted by nihilist groups. This essay borrows heavily from the concepts of French political theorist Jacques Bergie, but the author has adapted these concepts to write a provocative treatise on international terrorism.

Sterling, Claire. **The Terror Network: The Secret War of International Terrorism.** New York: Holt, Rinehart and Winston, 1981. 357p. ISBN 0-03-050661.

This book is one of the more famous books on European terrorist organizations, because charges have been made that the author had close connections with the CIA. The author's intent was to trace the international ties among terrorist organizations. Her thesis is that in its training of terrorists in Czechoslovakia in the 1970s the Soviet Union was responsible for most left-wing terrorist activity in Europe. This controversial book has its weaknesses, but it does express a viewpoint prevalent in U.S. government circles during the early 1980s.

Terrorist Organizations

Adams, James. **The Financing of Terror: How the Groups That Are Terrorizing the World Get the Money to Do It.** New York: Simon & Schuster, 1986. 293p. ISBN 0-671-49700-6.

A British journalist uses his news sources to trace how terrorist organizations finance their operations. He was able to interview leaders of terrorist organizations, who provided the author with insights that make this book invaluable. Among his more important conclusions is the financial stability of the PLO and its impact on PLO operations, the reluctance of terrorist groups to depend on the whimsical support of Qaddafi of Libya, and the cash-and-carry conditional backing of the former Soviet Union. This book is invaluable for both the material on financial aid given to terrorist organizations and the insights on how financial affairs affect terrorist operations.

Alexander, Yonah, and Alan O'Day, eds. **Terrorism in Ireland.** London: Croom Helm, 1984. 277p. ISBN 0-312-79260-3.

Thirteen specialists analyze modern Irish terrorism in Northern Ireland and Britain. The authors conclude that terrorism has been a longstanding Irish tactic against British forces and Protestants in Northern Ireland, and this is unlikely to change. Irish terrorists in the past have had few contacts with international terrorist groups, except for foreign weapons and financial aid from the United States, but this is liable to change.

Amos, John W. **Palestinian Resistance: Organization of a Nationalist Movement.** New York: Pergamon, 1980. 471p. ISBN 0-08-025094-7.

All aspects of the Palestinian resistance against Israel since 1948 are analyzed in this book. Israeli military successes and weaknesses among the Arabs have made the Palestinians resort to a mixture of diplomacy and terrorism. These tactics, however, have made it difficult to win the diplomatic and political war. This book is one of the few analytical approaches to the Palestinian problem, and it should be read for the analysis.

Becker, Jillian. **The PLO: The Rise and Fall of the Palestine Liberation Organization.** London: Weidenfeld and Nicolson, 1984. 303p. ISBN 0-297-78299-1.

A British terrorism specialist critiques the PLO and its supporters. His view is that the PLO has been a disaster for the Palestinian movement because of its record of mistaken political judgments and strategic errors. Becker believes the PLO has, from its inception, been an instrument of Arab politics and that it should dissolve itself. Despite the author's bias, this book has much to offer the reader in its insights into the leadership of the PLO.

Bethell, Nicholas. **The Palestine Triangle: The Struggle between the British, the Jews and the Arabs, 1935-48.** London: Deutsch, 1979. 384p. ISBN 0-233-97069-X.

This book traces the history of the Palestinian question through the British, Arab, and Jewish political maze of the late 1930s and 1940s. The author examines the role of Jewish terrorism and the extent to which it led to the British withdrawal from Palestine. Key British and Israeli participants have been interviewed by the author and their contributions put into historical perspective. The result is both a history of the last years of the British mandate in Palestine and an outline of a successful terrorist campaign.

Cobban, Helena. **The Palestinian Liberation Organisation: People, Power and Politics.** Cambridge: Cambridge University Press, 1984. 305p. ISBN 0-521-25128-1.

A detailed organizational study of the PLO by a British journalist. The analysis depends heavily upon interviews with the organization's principal leaders. The author identifies the PLO's main contributions to the Palestinian cause as its role in building Palestinian identity and its leadership in the guerrilla war with Israel. This book gives a good look at the leadership and goals of the PLO in the early 1980s.

Dillon, Sam. **Comandos: The CIA and Nicaragua's Contra Rebels.** New York: Henry Holt, 1991. 393p. ISBN 0-8050-1475-6.

A former reporter for the *Miami Herald* and a specialist on Latin American affairs writes on the relationship between the Contra rebels and the CIA in the war against the Sandinista regime in Nicaragua. The work is based largely on interviews with a leader of the Contra rebels, Luis Fley, who was both a battalion commander and an investigator of crimes committed by Contra fighters. The author concludes that the course of the war between the Contras and the Sandinistas was dictated by the CIA and the fighting ended when U.S. support ceased. Low-intensity warfare and terrorism occurred simultaneously in Nicaragua, and this book documents the connection.

Dobson, Christopher. **Black September: Its Short, Violent History.** New York: Macmillan, 1974. 179 pp. ISBN 0-02-531900-0.

The author was a journalist for the *Sunday Telegraph* (London) when he wrote this short history of the Palestinian terrorist group, Black September. He traces the background of the group and its connections with the Palestine Liberation Organization (PLO). Each of its terrorist operations are surveyed from its first assassination in Cairo in November 1971 to its last operation at Athens in August 1973. This book is a short, readable account of the PLO's most violent terrorism campaign.

Dobson, Christopher, and Ronald Payne. **The Carlos Complex: A Pattern of Violence.** London: Hodder and Stoughton, 1977. 254p. ISBN 0-340-2131-2.

The authors give terrorism a face by their interpretations of the terrorists operating in the mid-1970s. They concentrate on individual terrorists and their roles in the various terrorist organizations. The result is a collage of terrorism at its peak in the late 1960s and 1970s. While neither of the authors is sympathetic to the causes of terrorism or the individual terrorists, they provide a mass of useful information and insight about terrorism in that era.

Emerson, Steven A., and Cristina Del Sesto. **Terrorist: The Inside Story of the Highest Ranking Iraqi Terrorist Ever to Defect to the West.** New York: Villard Books, 1991. 233 pp. ISBN 0-679-73701-4.

Two American journalists interviewed the defector Adnan Awad, a former member of the Iraqi Abu Ibrahim terrorist organization. A Palestinian by birth, Awad was a key member of the Baghdad-based terrorist organization until his defection. While the authors often appear to be more interested in implicating the Bush administration for its blind support for Iraqi leader Saddam Hussein than in tracing the terrorist career of Awad, this biography still gives insight into the world of Middle East terrorism.

Flynn, Kevin, and Gary Gerhardt. **The Silent Brotherhood: Inside America's Racist Underground.** New York: Free Press, 1989. 419p. ISBN 0-02-910312-6.

The authors present a history of the American right-wing, racist, terrorist organization called the Silent Brotherhood. This group of about 15 terrorists was formed by Robert Jay Mathews in September 1983, and it existed until his death in December 1984. Each step in the Brotherhood's actions, from small-scale robberies and counterfeiting to murder and armored car robbery, is traced in detail by the authors. This book gives a good picture of the white supremacist movement in the United States, but the authors' practice of inserting their own dialogue brings the authors too much into the book.

Gowers, Andrew, and Tony Walker. **Behind the Myth: Yasser Arafat and the Palestinian Revolution.** New York: Olive Branch Press, 1991. 407 pp. ISBN 0-94073-86-5.

Two British journalists conducted an extensive series of interviews with PLO leader Arafat, his family, and friends in researching this political biography. Arafat has survived many crises and remains the embodiment of the Palestinian cause, but the deaths of able potential successors make the future uncertain for the PLO. The authors present a sympathetic view of the career of Arafat and his efforts to turn the PLO away from terrorism.

Gresh, Alain. **The PLO: The Struggle Within: Towards an Independent Palestinian State.** London: Zed Books, 1985. 267p. ISBN 0-86232-272-3.

The author presents a history of the PLO and the evolution of Palestinian political thinking about an independent Palestinian state. His book is based on PLO documents and interviews with PLO leaders. He believes that the PLO has made positive efforts to establish a secular Palestinian state, but the combination of internal disunity and the chaotic state of affairs after the Israeli invasion of Lebanon have made the future of the PLO uncertain. This book is a sympathetic treatment of the PLO, and it is a good place to study the organization's internal politics.

Hart, Alan. **Arafat: A Political Biography.** Bloomington: Indiana University Press, 1989. Rev. ed. 560 pp. ISBN 0-253-32711-3.

This book is a revised edition of the author's *Arafat, Terrorist or Peacemaker?* (1984) with material updated through 1989. The author, a British journalist, utilized his contacts in the Middle East to write a laudatory political biography of Yasser Arafat. He maintains that Arafat has done more than any other political leader to prepare the way for a long-lasting settlement of the Arab-Israeli conflict. Few books on Arafat are as positive toward him.

Heggoy, Alf Andrew. **Insurgency and Counterinsurgency in Algeria.** Bloomington: Indiana University Press, 1972. 327p. ISBN 0-253-33026-2.

This is an analysis of the Algerian struggle for independence from France in the late 1950s and early 1960s. Although the role of terrorism in this struggle is not the author's main concern, his treatment of the National Liberation Front (FLN) and its allies places terrorism and counterterrorism at the forefront. The ending of the war was a political settlement rather than the vanquishing of the French military, and terrorism was a tactic used by both sides. This book remains the best source on the terrorist organizations that operated in Algeria during that war.

Heskin, Ken. **Northern Ireland: A Psychological Analysis.** New York: Columbia University Press, 1980. 174p. ISBN 0-231-05138-7.

An Irish psychologist focuses on another dimension of the Northern Irish problem. His thesis is that terrorism in Northern Ireland is only the manifestation of deeper cultural, economic, and political problems. The Graduated Reciprocation in Tension-Reduction (GRIT) method of reducing political passions is the best approach available, but only time will tell if this approach will work. This book gives a good picture of the social and political environment in which terrorism still operates.

Hutchinson, Martha Crenshaw. **Revolutionary Terrorism: The FLN in Algeria, 1954–1962.** Stanford, CA: Hoover Institution Press, 1978. 178p. ISBN 0-8179-6961-6.

The author uses the historical example of the war of national liberation in Algeria (1954–1962) and the FLN terrorist organization to demonstrate how a successful terrorism campaign worked. Each use of terrorism is placed into the context of its contribution to the overthrow of the French in Algeria. The effective use of endorsement terrorism and compliance terrorism made the native Algerians support the revolution. This book is useful both for its analysis of terrorism and for its treatment of the Algerian-French war.

Kirisci, Kemal. **The PLO and World Politics: A Study of the Mobilization of Support for the Palestinian Cause.** London: Frances Pinter, 1986. 198p. ISBN 0-86187-585-0.

This work examines the position of the PLO in international politics. Special attention is given to the methods used by the PLO to establish itself as the representative of the Palestinians before the international community. By dramatizing the cause of the Palestinians and downplaying terrorism, the PLO scored an impressive diplomatic victory in the late 1970s and early 1980s. Some of the conclusions may need to be altered, but this book is still worth careful study.

Kurz, Anat, and Ariel Merari. **ASALA—Irrational Terror or Political Tool.** Jerusalem: Jaffee Center for Strategic Studies, 1985. 118p. ISBN 0-8133-0324-9.

Two Israeli authors present this study of the Armenian Secret Army for the Liberation of Armenia (ASALA). ASALA's terrorist activities have concentrated mainly on attacks against Turkish diplomats and property to avenge past Turkish repression of Armenians and to liberate Turkish Armenia. These terrorists claim that the recourse to terrorism has been justified because of past international indifference to the sufferings of the Armenian nation. This study is an effort to understand the motives and workings of a different kind of terrorist organization.

Lodge, Juliet, ed. **Terrorism: A Challenge to the State.** Oxford: Martin Robertson, 1981. 247p. ISBN 0-85520-297-1.

This book of essays includes case studies of international terrorism in various Western European countries. Each contributor analyzes the origin, organization, rationale, motives, and goals of the organizations in a particular country. This national approach to analyzing terrorism makes the book a valuable resource for studying terrorist groups in the early 1980s.

Melman, Yossi. **The Master Terrorist: The True Story behind Abu Nidal.** New York: Adama Books, 1986. 215p. ISBN 0-915361-52-3.

An Israeli author presents a biography of the infamous Palestinian terrorist Abu Nidal. Melman had access to several of Abu Nidal's relatives, and his account of the terrorist's background is one of the best features of the book. His details about Palestinian terrorist organizations are another positive feature. Little information is available on the lives of terrorists, and this biography is a welcome addition to the literature.

Merari, Ariel, and Shlomi Elad. **The International Dimension of Palestinian Terrorism.** Jerusalem: Jaffee Center for Strategic Studies, 1986. 147p. ISBN 0-8133-0458-X.

Two Israeli authors, both of whom are affiliated with the Jaffee Center for Strategic Studies Project on Terrorism, conclude that Palestinian groups have played a central role in international terrorism since 1968, but events in Lebanon in the mid-1980s curtailed Palestinian capabilities to strike at Israel. Palestinian terrorism will continue, however, because of the Abu Nidal group's commitment to terrorist tactics. While this book reflects an Israeli bias against Palestinian terrorists, it is still a good source because of the statistical data presented.

Mishal, Shaul. **The PLO under Arafat: Between Gun and Olive Branch.** New Haven, CT: Yale University Press, 1986. 190p. ISBN 0-300-03709-0.

Mishal traces Yasser Arafat's role in the PLO, concluding that his leadership made the PLO the sole legitimate representative of the Palestinian people, but that he has hindered further successes. The invasion of Lebanon and the subsequent mutiny in the PLO weakened Arafat's position.

Rapoport, David C., ed. **Inside Terrorist Organizations.** New York: Columbia University Press, 1988. 259p. ISBN 0-231-06720-8.

This book of essays presents a variety of ways to understand the operations of terrorist organizations. Some of the organizations, such as the Shining Path, have rarely been analyzed in other books on terrorism. The theoretical essays also provide several ways to reexamine terrorism. Each of these essays is a major contribution to the literature on terrorism.

Seale, Patrick. **Abu Nidal: A Gun for Hire.** New York: Random House, 1992. 339 pp. ISBN 0-679-40066-4.

The author, a British journalist specializing in Middle East politics, used his contacts within the PLO and information from defectors from the Abu Nidal Group to construct this political biography of Abu Nidal. Much of the personal information on Abu Nidal was given to him by the late Abu Iyad, the second in command of the PLO and Abu Nidal's former sponsor in the PLO. The author examines Iyad's thesis that Abu Nidal acts as an instrument of Israeli policy in his war against the leadership of the PLO and concludes that there may be some truth to this charge. This work is as important for its PLO sources as for the material on Abu Nidal.

Taheri, Amir. **Holy Terror: The Inside Story of Islamic Terrorism.** London: Hutchinson, 1987. 313p. ISBN 0-09-165970-1.

This book examines the nature and practice of terrorism by Islamic fundamentalist groups. Islamic terrorism is characterized by the author as rejecting all contemporary ideologies, conducting a Holy War without compromise, and embracing Islam both in individual conduct and for state policy. This brand of terrorism peaked in the mid-1980s, and many Muslims have since rejected Khomeini-type fundamentalism. This book is the best source on Islamic fundamentalist terrorism available.

Walter, Ingo. **Secret Money: The World of International Financial Secrecy.** London: Allen and Unwin, 1985. 213p. ISBN 0-04-332107-0.

The financial world of secret transactions is the subject of this book. International financial secrecy is imperative to the underworld of crime and international terrorist organizations, and though the international community has tried to control these funds, they have had only limited success. This book refers to terrorism only in passing, but it provides essential information on the financial systems behind international terrorism.

Weinberg, Leonard, and William Lee Eubank. **The Rise and Fall of Italian Terrorism.** Boulder, CO: Westview, 1987. 155p. ISBN 0-8133-0541-1.

The authors relate the history and development of neo-fascist and left-wing terrorist groups in Italy since World War II. A special feature is the biographies of 2,500 individuals who participated in terrorism. Finally, the steps taken by the Italian authorities to overcome the terrorist threat are studied in detail. This book is the most definitive treatment of Italian terrorism available.

Wilkinson, Paul. **The New Fascists.** London: Grant McIntyre, 1981. 179p. ISBN 0-86216-060-X.

This book examines right-wing terrorist organizations with a fascist orientation. Fascist and neo-Nazi parties have appeared in the postwar world, but because of electoral failures many of these groups have resorted to terrorist tactics. These groups' advocacy of racism causes the most damage to the democratic process.

Terrorist Incidents

Alexander, Yonah, and Kenneth A. Myers, eds. **Terrorism in Europe.** New York: St. Martin's, 1982. 216p. ISBN 0-312-79250-6.

These essays examine the various terrorist incidents in Europe during the last century. Most of the emphasis is on the 3,851 domestic and international terrorist operations that occurred in Europe from 1970 to 1981. The authors highlight the Italian, Spanish, and West German terrorist organizations. The essays range from historical examples to modern case studies.

Barker, Ralph. **Not Here, But in Another Place.** New York: St. Martin's, 1980. 356p. ISBN 0-312-57961-6.

This book is a popularized treatment of the South Moluccan terrorists' seizure of trains in The Netherlands in 1975 and 1977. Both the justifications for the train seizures by the South Moluccans and the reactions of the Dutch are covered in depth. This case study of a handful of terrorists attempting to dramatize their cause is worthy of consideration, since it is indicative of the typical motives behind terrorist acts.

Bar-Zohar, Michael, and Eitan Haber. **The Quest for the Red Prince.** New York: William Morrow, 1983. 232p. ISBN 0-688-02043-7.

Two Israeli writers chronicle the career of the Palestinian terrorist Ali Hassan Salameh. Salameh's father was killed fighting the Israelis in the 1948 war, and his son continued to fight against Israel by becoming one of the leaders of Black September. An Israeli counterterrorism team finally assassinated Salameh in West Beirut in 1979, but not before he had conducted several bloody terrorist operations against Israeli targets. The pro-Israeli bias of this book is apparent, but the story of the life of Salameh is illustrative of the environment that breeds terrorism.

Blundy, David, and Andrew Lycett. **Qaddafi and the Libyan Revolution.** Boston: Little, Brown, 1987. 230p. ISBN 0-316-10042-0.

Colonel Qaddafi's sponsorship of terrorism has long been documented, but this book traces the rise of Qaddafi as Libya's leader and the reasons for his involvement in terrorism. The authors maintain that Qaddafi has little liking or respect for Western institutions and political practices. Despite his geographical remoteness from the Palestinian conflict, Qaddafi sponsors terrorism both out of personal commitment to the Arab cause and for political advantage. Qaddafi has always been a puzzle to Westerners, and this book gives some insight into one of the key players in the Middle East quagmire.

Carlson, Kurt. **One American Must Die: A Hostage's Personal Account of the Hijacking of Flight 847.** New York: Congdon and Weed, 1986. 172p. ISBN 0-86553-161-7.

The author, a passenger on the hijacked aircraft TWA Flight 847 in 1985, gives a personal account of the events. Most of the hostages were released, but Carlson, returning from a military mission in Egypt, was held first by the Amal in Beirut and then by the Syrians before the Israelis made a deal by releasing 735 Shi'ite prisoners. Although the author was never mistreated by the hijackers, the death of a fellow hostage and the uncertainty of future treatment made him wonder if he would survive the experience. This book gives the participant's viewpoint only; it should be read in conjunction with a work on the politics of aircraft hijacking.

Coyle, Dominick J. **Minorities in Revolt: Political Violence in Ireland, Italy, and Cyprus.** London: Associated University Presses, 1983. 253p. ISBN 0-8386-3120-7.

The author uses three national case studies to support his thesis that a group of people excluded from normal governing processes will often resort to politically motivated violence. His case studies are Ireland, Italy, and Cyprus. These are areas where the author has spent considerable time during his career as a journalist. This book takes a different approach to the study of terrorism, and is an interesting contribution.

Emerson, Steven, and Brian Duffy. **The Fall of Pan Am 103: Inside the Lockerbie Investigation.** New York: Putnam, 1990. 304p. ISBN 0-399-13521-9.

Two American journalists, editors at *U.S. News & World Report,* give an inside story of the destruction of Pan Am Fight 103 over Lockerbie, Scotland, in 1988 and its subsequent investigation. They focus both on the actual event and the lengthy investigation with all its pitfalls. The authors conclude that certain aspects of this act of terrorism will never be uncovered. This book is a readable treatment of one of the most famous terrorist incidents in this century.

Katz, Robert. **Days of Wrath: The Ordeal of Aldo Moro: The Kidnapping, the Execution, the Aftermath.** Garden City, NY: Doubleday, 1980. 326p. ISBN 0-385-14910-7.

The author gives a detailed sketch of the politics of the abduction and murder of former Italian prime minister Aldo Moro. He shows that the intransigent policies of the Italian authorities backfired because of the skillful use of Moro by the Red Brigade. Moro's death was unnecessary, but the Italian government used it as a way to attack the terrorists. The gradual unfolding of the political drama by the author, who was in Italy throughout the crisis, makes this a good case study of the paralyzing effect of terrorism.

Salinger, Pierre. **America Held Hostage: The Secret Negotiations.** Garden City, NY: Doubleday, 1981. 349p. ISBN 0-385-17750-X.

An American journalist active behind the scenes of the negotiations gives the story of the Iranian hostage crisis and the diplomacy behind the release of the hostages. His treatment intertwines personalities and events before, during, and after the seizure of the American embassy. The cultural gap between the U.S. government and Iran's revolutionary leadership was never bridged, and this prolonged the crisis. Despite the journalistic flavor of this book, it constitutes a solid assessment of the hostage crisis.

Weir, Ben, and Carol Weir. **Hostage Bound, Hostage Free.** Philadelphia: Westminster, 1987. 182p. ISBN 0-664-21322-7.

This book is the story of the kidnapping of protestant minister Ben Weir in Beirut in May 1984, and his ordeal as a hostage. While Weir was held by Shi'ite terrorists for more than two years, his wife worked with U.S. government officials to win his release. The Shi'ites, attempting to win the release of their own terrorists in Kuwait, let Weir go in September 1986 to serve as a messenger. This book gives a look at the life of a hostage held by Shi'ite terrorists and the efforts of relatives to put pressure on various governments to gain his freedom.

State Terrorism

Adelman, Jonathan R., ed. **Terror and Communist Politics: The Role of the Secret Police in Communist States.** Boulder, CO: Westview, 1984. 292p. ISBN 0-86531-293-1.

This is a collection of scholarly case studies on how Communist regimes used terror to control their people. The secret police in former Soviet bloc countries performed a variety of functions, but their focus was on stabilization of the Communist regimes. This book provides insights on the effectiveness of state terror in silencing potential dissidents even in regimes collapsing from internal economic and political stresses.

Fisher, Jo. **Mothers of the Disappeared.** Boston: South End, 1989. 168p. ISBN 0-89608-371-3.

This book presents interviews with the mothers of persons who disappeared in the counterterrorist crackdown by the Argentine government during the late 1970s. Thousands of suspected dissidents were tortured and murdered by government forces. Each interview is preceded by a short synopsis of the political environment at the time the individual was taken away by the authorities. This book fills a void in understanding how state terrorism uses the military and police to control opposition.

Hodges, Donald C. **Argentina's "Dirty War": An Intellectual Biography.** Austin: University of Texas Press, 1991. 387p. ISBN 0-292-70423-2.

An American professor of philosophy and political science surveys Argentine politics during the period of the "dirty war" (1975–1978) and the military repression (1976–1982) to find the roots of the conflict. He concludes that the terrorist campaign from the political left and the counterterrorist operations from the political right represented the culmination of social tensions arising out of Argentina's political past. A major part of his thesis is that a resurgence of revolutionary terrorism and corresponding state terrorism is possible in Argentina because the social tensions remain. While this book is intended to be an intellectual history of Argentine politics between 1975 and 1982, it also tells us much about terrorism and counterterrorism during this period.

O'Kane, Rosemary H. T. **The Revolutionary Reign of Terror: The Role of Violence in Political Change.** Aldershot, England: Edward Elgar, 1991. 304p. ISBN 1-85278-082-7.

A British academic contributes new insights in her study of the various reigns of terror by states in the midst of revolution. Besides the French Revolution and the Russian Revolution, the author studies China (1949), Cuba (1959), Ethiopia (1976–1978), Iran (1979–1982), and Nicaragua (1979) as modern examples to support her thesis that revolutionary reigns of terror are similar in their use of summary justice. She emphasizes the importance of civil wars in pushing revolutionary authorities to resort to terror to defend the revolution.

Perdue, William D. **Terrorism and the State: A Critique of Domination through Fear.** New York: Praeger, 1989. 229p. ISBN 0-275-93140-4.

The author, an American professor of sociology, takes a critical look at state terrorism. He is alarmed at the one-sided view of terrorism currently held by specialists. State terrorism is at least as serious a problem on the international scene as the terrorism of European left-wing or Palestinian groups. This is a thoughtful analysis of the ramifications of state terrorism.

Simpson, John, and Jana Bennett. **The Disappeared and the Mothers of the Plaza: The Story of the 11,000 Argentinians Who Vanished.** New York: St. Martin's, 1985. 416p. ISBN 0-312-21229-1.

Two British journalists conducted research during 1983 and 1984 for this book on state terrorism in Argentina. Their thesis is that the Argentine government waged a war between 1976 and 1983 that was intended not simply to wipe out terrorism, but rather to end potential opposition of any kind. The regime eventually collapsed due to the military defeat in the Falklands War and a weak domestic economy, not because of any public reaction to the government's terrorism. This book is a popular but thorough treatment of a frightening case of state terrorism.

Stohl, Michael, and George A. Lopez, eds. **The State as Terrorist: The Dynamics of Governmental Violence and Repression.** Westport, CT: Greenwood, 1984. 202p. ISBN 0-313-12726-3.

This collection of essays concerns the use of violence, repression, and terrorism by the state in the pursuit of domestic and international goals.

Technological, Chemical, and Biological Terrorism

Alexander, Yonah, and Charles K. Ebinger, eds. **Political Terrorism and Energy: The Threat and Response.** New York: Praeger, 1982. 258p. ISBN 0-03-059344-1.

This book of essays focuses on the terrorist threat to international energy sources. The authors are concerned about terrorist attacks on utilities and oil installations, but major attention is devoted to the prospect of nuclear terrorism. While no measures can insure absolute security of any energy logistical system, the authors agree that remote siting of plants and other preventive measures will help. Although many of the essays may be considered alarmist, the contributors have produced serious essays on the possibility of terrorist activities against energy facilities.

Clark, Richard Charles. **Technological Terrorism.** Old Greenwich, CT: Devin-Adair, 1980. 220p. ISBN 0-8159-6915-5.

This book concerns technological terrorism, or the seizure and use of weapons of mass destruction by terrorist groups. Weapons of mass destruction include nuclear arms and chemical and biological weapons. The author maintains that technological terrorism constitutes a present danger.

Hoffman, Bruce. **Terrorism in the United States and the Potential Threat to Nuclear Facilities.** Santa Monica, CA: Rand Corporation, 1986. 56p.

This Rand Corporation report examines the threat by terrorists to U.S. nuclear weapons facilities. While the United States has been immune from terrorist attacks in the past and the terrorist threat to U.S. nuclear weapons facilities remains low, a threat does exist. Symbolic bombings in pursuit of political goals rather than large-scale attacks on defended sites are the standard practice of domestic terrorists. The Rand Corporation produces these reports for U.S. government agencies, and this report is a balanced assessment of possible terrorist activity against nuclear facilities.

Leventhal, Paul, and Yonah Alexander, eds. **Nuclear Terrorism: Defining the Threat.** Washington, DC: Pergamon-Brasseys, 1986. 218p. ISBN 0-08-034323-6.

These papers are the result of a multidisciplinary conference on the threat of nuclear terrorism held in Washington, D.C., in 1985. The themes of the conference were defining the threat of nuclear terrorism and outlining the efforts necessary to counteract this threat. Most of the authors grant that nuclear terrorism is a growing possibility because of the fanaticism of the terrorists and the increasingly easy access of them to nuclear materials. Both the papers and the commentaries delve deeply into this issue, and the resulting collection is a solid contribution to the literature on this subject.

Leventhal, Paul, and Yonah Alexander, eds. **Preventing Nuclear Terrorism: The Report and Papers of the International Task Force on Prevention of Nuclear Terrorism.** Lexington, MA: Lexington Books, 1987. 472p. ISBN 0-669-14884-9.

The International Task Force is a panel of 26 nuclear policy experts from nine countries whose purpose is to assess the vulnerabilities of civil and military nuclear programs to terrorism. While these experts find the probability of nuclear terrorism remote, they note that the possibility of terrorists acquiring the know-how and the necessary raw materials is increasing. Recommendations include the reduction of the production of weapon-usable forms of plutonium and uranium, and the adoption of self-protecting systems. This report and the following articles make this book one of the top sources on nuclear terrorism available.

Terrorism and the Former Soviet Union

Cline, Ray S., and Yonah Alexander. **Terrorism: The Soviet Connection.** New York: Crane, Russak, 1984. 162p. ISBN 0-8448-1471-7.

The ongoing connection between international terrorism and the policy of destabilization by the Soviet Union is the theme of this book by two American experts. They claim that the extent to which the Soviet Union sponsored and controlled terrorism by supplying arms and money to terrorist organizations makes it impossible to dispute Soviet responsibility for terrorism. The only way to control terrorist activities is for the United States to launch a full-scale counterattack against terrorism and wars of national liberation, according to the authors. Many of the conclusions are now dated, but the information on Soviet sponsorship of terrorism during the 1960s and 1970s is still useful.

Golan, Galia. **Gorbachev's "New Thinking" on Terrorism.** New York: Praeger, 1990. 117p. ISBN 0-275-93482-9.

An Israeli expert on terrorism analyzes what she perceives as a major shift in Soviet policy toward terrorism under Mikhail Gorbachev. While Soviet leadership was never comfortable with terrorism, except with the instance of wars of national liberation, Gorbachev instituted an unprecedented policy of greater cooperation with the Western democracies in preventing international terrorism. This cooperation should not be overrated, but the author felt that it was still a positive sign of the weakening of Soviet support for terrorism. Subsequent events in the early 1990s have proven the contentions of the author in this book, and the book should be read in this light.

Goren, Roberta. **The Soviet Union and Terrorism.** London: Allen and Unwin, 1984. 232p. ISBN 0-04-327073-5.

This book is a study of international terrorism as an instrument of policy by the Soviet Union. The author concludes that "active support of international terrorism in countries outside the Soviet bloc has been part of Soviet government policy since 1917 and is consistent with Soviet ideology." This sponsorship of terrorism by the Soviet Union was always a useful option in its strategy to destabilize the West. Recent research has modified most of the conclusions of this book, but the book is a good example of the type of anti-Soviet propaganda current in Western circles in the 1970s and early 1980s.

Terrorism and the Media

Clutterbuck, Richard. **The Media and Political Violence.** London: Macmillan, 1981. 191p. ISBN 0-333-31484-0.

This examination of the relationship between political violence and the news media criticizes the media for publicizing terrorism and thereby encouraging more violence. Clutterbuck's conclusion is that the journalistic profession should establish a disciplinary body to enforce journalistic ethics. While this book is controversial in many of its points, it is worth reading for the same reason.

Schmid, Alex P., and Janny de Graaf. **Violence as Communication: Insurgent Terrorism and the Western News Media.** London: Sage, 1982. 283p. ISBN 0-8039-9789-2.

Two Dutch media specialists have combined to produce this book on terrorism, news, and political and public responses. By placing terrorist and media practices from various times and places into a comparative perspective, the authors seek to gain insight on their common properties. They believe that insurgent terrorism should be viewed as communication toward an end rather than mere violence, and the news media is the means of communication. This book should be required reading for students of the media and terrorism.

Counterterrorism

Chapman, Robert D., and M. Lester Chapman. **The Crimson Web of Terror.** Boulder, CO: Paladin, 1980. 155p. ISBN 0-87364-187-6.

The primary author was a member of the Central Intelligence Agency (CIA) for 27 years, and his specialty was counterterrorism planning. This book relates his experience with terrorist operations. He concludes that terrorism is a form of insurgency that can be defeated by counterinsurgency tactics. The value of this book is in the author's experience with terrorism and the viewpoints he has adopted from it.

Clutterbuck, Richard. **The Future of Political Violence: Destabilization Disorder and Terrorism.** Houndmills, England: Macmillan, 1986. 206p. ISBN 0-333-37989-6.

Both the essays and a long overview by the author originate from a conference on political violence in 1983 that was sponsored jointly by the Royal United Services Institute (RUSI) and Control Risks Information Services (CRIS). This combination produced a list of contributors from the armed forces, police, civil service, and the business world. The main theme is the need for security against and control of violence from terrorists.

Clutterbuck, Richard. **Guerrillas and Terrorists.** Athens: Ohio University Press, 1980. 125p. ISBN 0-8214-0590-X.

The intent in this work is to promote understanding and cooperation among the police, the general public, and the media in combating terrorism. This book is a product of six Lees-Knowles Lectures at Cambridge University in 1975–1976. Despite its mid-1970s framework, it is still valuable in outlining theories of ways to discourage terrorism.

Cole, Richard B. **Executive Security: A Corporate Guide to Effective Response to Abduction and Terrorism.** New York: Wiley, 1980. 323p. ISBN 0-471-07736-4.

A law enforcement specialist details the steps necessary to forestall abduction of business executives. While most of the analysis is directed toward prevention, the author has several sections on victim recovery. The thrust of the author's argument is that all medium-to-large corporations need an ongoing program on executive security, for which this book provides a manual.

Dobson, Christopher, and Ronald Payne. **Terror! The West Fights Back.** London: Macmillan, 1982. 218p. ISBN 0-333-29417-3.

This is a popularized account of international terrorism and the measures undertaken by Western countries to counter it. The authors believe that the West has had terrorism on the defensive since 1981 because of closer cooperation and the development of effective counterterrorism policies. They approve of the firmer approach toward terrorism by the Reagan administration. Subsequent events have proven them wrong on certain points, but it is still a book worth looking at for its viewpoints.

Flood, Susan, ed. **International Terrorism: Policy Implications.** Chicago: University of Illinois at Chicago, Office of International Criminal Justice, 1991. 195p. ISBN 0-942551-35-2.

The authors of these essays represent both the practitioner's and researcher's perspectives on international terrorism. Most of the essays are brief analyses of specific problems, such as Cuba's role in narco-terrorism, the Japanese Red Army, chemical and biological terrorism, terrorism in Latin America, and the bombing of La Belle Discotheque, among others.

Gal-Or, Noemi. **International Cooperation to Suppress Terrorism.** London: Croom Helm, 1985. ISBN 0-70993813-6.

The author, an Israeli specialist on terrorism, claims that international cooperation among the Western countries is the key to controlling political terrorism. While the European Community's European Convention on the Suppression of Terrorism in 1979 was a step in the right direction, the convention's weaknesses have hindered the war against terrorism. This book is both a theoretical and a practical approach to terrorism, but it is most useful for its assessment of legal issues.

Hewitt, Christopher. **The Effectiveness of Anti-Terrorist Policies.** Lanham, MD: University Press of America, 1984. 122p. ISBN 0-8191-4254-9.

This book surveys policies that have been used against urban terrorism and evaluates their effectiveness. Five cases are selected: the IRA in Northern Ireland (1970–1981), ETA in Spain (1975–1981), Red Brigade in Italy (1977–1981), Tupamaros in Uruguay (1968–1973), and EOKA in Cyprus (1955–1958). By utilizing time-series analysis, the author measures the effectiveness of antiterrorist policies, showing that some policies are successful in certain situations and not in others. This book is a good introduction to antiterrorism.

Kupperman, Robert, and Jeff Kamen. **Final Warning: Averting Disaster in the New Age of Terrorism.** New York: Doubleday, 1989. 249p. ISBN 0-385-24584-X.

Two American experts document the terrorist threat to the United States. Every conceivable terrorist threat to the U.S. government and public is examined in detail with the warning that terrorists are planning to expand terrorism to the North American continent. The authors are disheartened by the lack of preparation for this threat. While widespread terrorism has yet to be introduced into the United States, this book shows how vulnerable this country is to a sustained terrorist campaign.

Livingstone, Neil C., and Terrell E. Arnold, eds. **Fighting Back: Winning the War against Terrorism.** Lexington, MA: Lexington Books, 1986. 268p. ISBN 0-669-10808-1.

These essays deal with international terrorism and the steps necessary to defeat this threat to U.S. national security. The authors claim that terrorism represents a cheap and effective weapon of warfare against the United States and its allies. To counter this strategy, the Western democracies need to change from a reactive posture to an aggressive strategy against terrorism. This book is an attempt to answer questions about methods to eliminate international terrorism, but it succeeds more in pointing out the difficulties of dealing with terrorism.

Motley, James B. **U.S. Strategy to Counter Domestic Political Terrorism.** Washington, DC: National Defense University Press, 1983. 136p.

This book assesses the state security preparations to prevent terrorism from spreading to the U.S. government. The author believes that public apathy toward terrorism makes it a threat to domestic security. Current antiterrorism strategy among U.S. authorities is reactive, and the author recommends that a more aggressive strategy be adopted under the supervision of a central agency. While the terrorist threat has not developed as dramatically as the author envisaged, his recommendations are still relevant.

Rubin, Barry, ed. **The Politics of Counterterrorism: The Ordeal of Democratic States.** Washington, DC: The Johns Hopkins University Foreign Policy Institute, 1990. 222p. ISBN 0-941700-60-7.

This book of essays on counterterrorism topics was published to further public understanding of the threat of international terrorism to democratic states. American and French experts on terrorism use case studies from Colombia, France, Italy, Japan, and the United States to reinforce this thesis. Special emphasis is on how individual countries have developed a public consensus on counterterrorist policies. This book provides a forum to study various case studies on the effectiveness of counterterrorism strategies.

St. John, Peter. **Air Piracy, Airport Security, and International Terrorism: Winning the War against Hijackers.** New York: Quorum Books, 1991. 280p. ISBN 0-89930-413-3.

A Canadian terrorism scholar surveys the history of air piracy by terrorists and the steps taken by airport security to end aircraft hijackings. He is careful to note the trends in aircraft hijackings and explain them in a concise way. Intelligence is the key to fighting international terrorism, and the Lockerbie incident showed that cooperation between security forces is imperative. This book is a good summary of current ideas on the prevention of air piracy, and the charts, graphs, and tables at the end of the book are especially valuable.

Siljander, Raymond P. **Terrorist Attacks: A Protective Service Guide for Executives, Bodyguards and Policemen.** Springfield, IL: Charles C. Thomas, 1980. 328p. ISBN 0-398-04028-1.

The author has used his security and law enforcement experience to produce a manual for the protection of potential targets of terrorist attacks. He outlines the ways terrorists strike and the best methods to prevent or thwart such attacks. This manual has much information on specific tactics to hinder terrorist attacks. Despite its concentration on prevention, this book offers useful profiles of terrorist groups.

Sloan, Stephen. **Simulating Terrorism.** Norman: University of Oklahoma Press, 1981. 158p. ISBN 0-80611-746-X.

Simulation theory is used by the author as the basis for a study of terrorism and ways to combat it. His intent is to utilize the knowledge gained from past terrorist activities to assist those charged with meeting the threat of future terrorism. His conclusion is that American law enforcement agencies are ill-equipped to handle the small, tightly organized terrorist groups because of administrative entanglements and the lack of coherent policies. Sloan offers a critical look at counterterrorist programs in the United States.

Tophoven, Rolf. **GSG9: German Response to Terrorism.** Koblenz, Germany: Bernard und Graefe Verlag, 1984. 124p. ISBN 3-7637-5446-6.

The former West German counterterrorism unit, GSG9 of the Federal German Border Guard (BGS), is surveyed for its training, equipment, and organization. This unit became famous for its 1977 operations at the Mogadishu Airport in Somalia. Besides information about the composition of this unit, the author gives a complete list of special command and combat equipment. This book shows the importance of antiterrorist operations undertaken by the West Germans since the 1972 Munich Olympics incident. GSG9 still exists in the reunified Germany.

Wilkinson, Paul. **British Perspectives on Terrorism.** London: Allen and Unwin, 1981. 193p. ISBN 0-04-327064-6.

British research on international and national terrorism is represented in this book of essays. From experience with terrorism in colonial wars and in Northern Ireland, the British have had to adjust to terrorist activities. These essays range from the methods that the British developed to counter terrorism to intragovernment efforts to control international terrorism. Such essays are an excellent introduction to the ways that the British have learned to cope with terrorist threats.

Wolf, John B. **Fear of Fear: A Survey of Terrorist Operations and Controls in Open Societies.** New York: Plenum, 1981. 235p. ISBN 0-305-40766-3.

This is a survey of the techniques and tactics used by international terrorist groups, and methods necessary to bring terrorism under control. Most of the useful parts of this book come from the author's recommendations on ways to curtail political terrorism. The author intended this book is serve as an antiterrorist manual.

Yallop, H. J. **Protection against Terrorism.** Chichester, England: Barry Rose, 1980. 92p. ISBN 0-85992-202-2.

The author presents his views on defensive measures to prevent terrorist bombing attacks. These attacks tend to occur in waves regardless of the country or cause. The author is less interested in bomb disposal than the principles of identification and other preventive measures. No other source on the market has the information available in this book.

Political Hostages

Aston, Clive C. **A Contemporary Crisis: Political Hostage-Taking and the Experience of Western Europe.** Westport, CT: Greenwood, 1982. 217p. ISBN 0-313-23289-X.

The response of national government to political hostage incidents is the subject of this book, based on a study of 127 hostage incidents in Western Europe between 1970 and 1980. The author concludes that the nature of a hostage incident will determine the crisis management mode of the government. This book is the best available source on government options in hostage situations.

Cooper, H. H. A. **The Hostage-Takers.** Boulder, CO: Paladin, 1981. 82p. ISBN 0-87364-209-0.

The author is a consultant on safety and survival techniques whose specialty is working with hostage-taking incidents. He has written a training text about the type of individuals who engage in hostage seizures and the methods used by them to accomplish their goals. He contends there is nothing new in hostage-taking, and simple precautions can prevent most incidents. This book is the best source on hostage-taking available.

Eichelman, Burr, David Soskis, and William Reid, eds. **Terrorism: Interdisciplinary Perspectives.** Washington, DC: American Psychiatric Association, 1983. 186p. ISBN 0-89042-109-9.

These papers are the outcome of a symposium on terrorism and hostage situations that was held at Cross Keys, Maryland, in September 1979. Psychiatrists and law enforcement officers gathered to discuss the role psychiatrists should play in events during and after hostage-taking incidents. The consensus among the authors is that the best role of psychiatry is to help terrorism victims recover. This book offers a number of solid papers on the psychological aftermath of a terrorist incident.

Jenkins, Brian M. **Embassies under Siege: A Review of 48 Embassy Takeovers, 1971–1980.** Santa Monica, CA: Rand Corporation 1981. 38p. ISBN 0-8330-295-3.

This Rand report is a study of embassy seizures and attempted seizures during 1971–1980. These takeovers were attempted by both small terrorist teams and large groups of militants. Successful takeovers have declined in recent years, partly because of increased embassy security. This report is a high-quality effort by one of the Rand Corporation's foremost experts on terrorism.

Jenkins, Brian M., ed. **Terrorism and Personal Protection.** Boston: Butterworth, 1985. 451p. ISBN 0-409-95126-9.

A group of specialists on security and terrorism present essays on terrorist kidnappings, providing a reference volume for those interested in personal security in a potential terrorist setting. All aspects of kidnapping—the threat, seizure, and negotiations—are covered by these essays. This book is an excellent source for information and statistical data on terrorist kidnappings.

Miller, Abraham H. **Terrorism and Hostage Negotiations.** Boulder, CO: Westview, 1980. 134p. ISBN 0-89158-856-6.

This book treats the hostage negotiations aspect of terrorism. Most of the interpretation comes from a detailed analysis of specific cases and interviews with government and law enforcement personnel. Some of the author's predictions of increased terrorist activity during the 1980s proved wrong, but the analysis of hostage negotiations is first-rate.

Legal Responses to Terrorism

Cassese, Antonio. **Terrorism, Politics and Law: The *Achille Lauro* Affair.** Princeton, New Jersey: Princeton University Press, 1989. 162p. ISBN 0-691-0738-6.

An Italian lawyer uses the legal issues surrounding the hijacking of the tourist cruise ship *Achille Lauro* in 1985 to study the relationship between terrorism and international law. His conclusions are that despite irregularities in the administration of international agreements by Egypt and Italy, the hijacking of the terrorists by the United States was the biggest legal mistake by any of the participants. Precedent for this action was lacking, and the United States has established and maintains a dangerous practice. This is a legalistic treatment of a complex case in international law.

Council of Europe, Parliamentary Assembly. **Conference on the Defence of Democracy against Terrorism in Europe: Tasks and Problems.** Strasbourg, France: Council of Europe, 1981. ca. 250p.

This book of documents, reports, and papers is the product of a conference on democracy and terrorism held in Strasbourg in 1980, sponsored jointly by the Council of Europe Assembly's Political Affairs Committee and its Legal Affairs Committee. The intent of the conference was to study terrorism and make proposals to the Council of Europe for legal countermeasures. While most of this material concerns European terrorism, the results can apply to other areas of the world. This book has a unique accumulation of documents and viewpoints on terrorism unavailable in any other source.

Ferencz, Benjamin B. **An International Criminal Court: A Step toward World Peace—A Documentary History and Analysis.** 2 vols. London: Oceana, 1980. ISBN 0-379-20390-1.

The author of this two-volume set advocates an international criminal court as the most effective way to control terrorism. Volume I examines earlier international court efforts to handle international crimes beginning with the Hague Conferences and ending with the Nuremberg and Tokyo war crime trials. In Volume II, the author presents his recommendations for an international criminal court to handle international terrorism as well as other international crimes. Besides the arguments in the text, the value of this work resides in the supporting documents.

Murphy, John F. **Punishing International Terrorists: The Legal Framework for Policy Initiatives.** Totowa, NJ: Rowman and Allanheld, 1985. 142p. ISBN 0-8476-7449-5.

The law enforcement effort to apprehend, prosecute, and (if convicted) punish the terrorist is the focus of this brief book by an American legal scholar. Punishment as a deterrence to terrorism is analyzed by the author for its effectiveness. The author recommends revision of American extradition legislation, revision of bilateral extradition treaties to conform to the U.S.–Costa Rica model, and some use of the UN and international courts for international legislation on terrorism. This book fills a void as a legal treatise on the punishment of terrorists.

Ronzitti, Natalino. **Rescuing Nationals Abroad through Military Co-ercion and Intervention on Grounds of Humanity.** Dordrecht, The Netherlands: Martinus Nijhoff, 1985. 216p. ISBN 90-247-3135-6.

This book studies military intervention for the protection of citizens abroad and for humanitarian purposes. Emphasis is on the legal restraints to military intervention on humanitarian grounds. The author is more concerned with interpretations of international law than about the ethics of intervention in terrorist incidents. This book resembles a sourcebook because of its objective treatment of the legal issues surrounding the rescuing of nationals in foreign countries.

Index